JUST BETWEEN US

Our Private Diary

PHOTOGRAPHY AND CREATIVE DIRECTION BY DEAN FREEMAN

INTRODUCTION

It seems hard to believe that just a few years ago we were queuing up for the *X Factor* auditions, hoping to be noticed, dreaming about getting a record deal one day. So much has happened since then! We've been on the most incredible journey and been caught up in a whirlwind of performing, touring, writing, recording and meeting our fans, not to mention the occasional party or two . . .

But you know what? We've been going so fast that it's been hard to keep track of everything we've been doing; when we look back, the last couple of years sometimes seem like a big jumble of memories. So in April 2009 we decided to start keeping a diary, so that we can remember all the fantastic times we've experienced and recall exactly how we felt as they were happening.

Most of all, we wanted to share the most amazing year of our lives with you, our fans, who have made it all possible. There have been so many milestones: our first single, our first number one, our number one album, two MOBO Awards, two Brit Awards . . . it's just so hard to believe! We want to say a huge thank you to everyone who bought our records, came to see us perform and supported us in the way that only JLS fans can. Hope you enjoy the book. We love you all!

Good Ol' Wossy ! Ha hehe...

1   COUNTDOWN . . .

• **ORITSÉ** Today we're recording 'Beat Again', our first single. It's a great song, so it's funny to think that Marvin and I were the only ones who liked it at first. Aston wasn't really feeling it, but I just loved it. I like those vibes. It's forward thinking, quite new-school, and I'm more than happy to have it as the first song. It fits our identity.

For ages I was sure that 'Everybody In Love' would be our first single, and so were Marvin and Aston. But a couple of months ago, JB said, 'It's going to be "Beat Again".'

'Do you really think so?' I said.

'Trust me,' he said. 'Wait and see.'

He always says, 'Trust me,' and he usually ends up being right.

• **MARVIN** We first heard 'Beat Again' when we were on tour with *The X Factor*. It was one of the last songs we were sent. There was one line that really stood out for me in the lyrics: 'If I died, would you come to my funeral?' I questioned it at first. Should you be talking about funerals in a love song? But it's a great song with some great images: 'I need love CPR' is really clever.

Several writers and producers sent us songs to consider and 'Everybody In Love' was one of the first to come through. We all thought it would work as a great first song, but the record company wanted to go with 'Beat Again'. I hope it's the right decision. You have to trust these guys; they know the industry inside out. But what if they're wrong?

• **ASTON** When we heard the demo for 'Beat Again', somebody else was singing it and I just wasn't convinced. The sound of the music was fresh and current and the lyrical content was clever, but it didn't jump out at me like 'Forever And A Day', which is what 'Everybody In Love' was originally called. The first time I heard that, I was like, 'Wow!' It really had a goose-bump effect.

It wasn't until I heard 'Beat Again' with us singing on it that I knew it was a powerful song. That was a lesson: if somebody says, 'This is a good track,' then give it a chance. You never know, you could enjoy singing it and really like it afterwards.

But 'Forever And A Day' was still our favourite song, which was why we wanted to release it first. Then our management said, 'Why not go in with an up-tempo song, one that everyone is loving, and then hit the fans with something they have never heard before?' It made sense.

• **JB** I got back from holiday this morning and came straight to the studio for 11am! Had a great time in Antigua and I've recharged my batteries. We listened to three different mixes of 'Beat Again' today and after taking the intro out, changing the instruments on some parts and making a few additions, it sounds wicked. It's ready to go!

• **ASTON** The original brief from the label was that the lead singer should be me, but that's not the way things work anymore. We are out of *The X Factor*, in a new phase of our career, and we're going back to our old methods of working with whatever sounds right. Today, Steve Mac and I recorded the whole song first. (Steve wrote 'Beat Again', along with Wayne Hector.) I sang all the parts: the first verse, the bridge, the chorus, the second verse, the middle eight, all of it. I was in there for ages!

'Pick out the bits you like,' Steve said. I knew immediately that some parts didn't suit my voice as well as they suited Oritsé's, JB's or Marvin's. The others came in and recorded various parts and in the end we decided that Oritsé starts the song. I do the bridge, we all do the chorus, then Marvin does the second verse. I come in with a bridge and JB sings the middle eight, then we all sing the chorus. It is a good mix – it has worked out perfectly.

friday 8 may
In the studio with Steve Mac

• **MARVIN** 'Beat Again' was on Radio 1 today! Just one week since we recorded it! It's crazy how quickly the track's been turned around, from the studio to the radio. We knew it was going to get played, but we didn't know it was going to be that fast. It's a really weird feeling. Our first single! It's set to be released around the middle of July.

• JB As much as you put the work in behind the scenes, or you play it at home and think it sounds good, it's different when somebody else plays it. After all, they don't *have* to play it; they're playing it because they like it! Steve put the radio on through the speakers in the studio and we all went mad. It's never going to sound the same as it does when you play it at home and turn the speakers up; music sounds different on the radio because it is compressed. But it's incredible, all the same.

thursday 14 may

• JB 'Beat Again' was requested on Capital today. I heard it in the car! It gives me a really weird feeling to think that there are so many people listening to the song, requesting it on radio stations. I wonder if I'll ever get used to it?

friday 29 may
At the Metrophonic Studios in Surrey

• **MARVIN** We're having a really creative time. We've written five songs in two days and they're all fantastic! It's great doing something so different from interviews and performing. JB's really enjoying himself, because writing songs is his favourite part of the job.

This place used to be a farm before it was converted to studios. It has a football pitch, tennis courts and a swimming pool – it's really cool. You just turn up and feel like you are on a retreat. It's like a boot camp for songwriters. Every part of the farm is a studio: there are two in the main house and three in the out-buildings. The creative juices are really flowing! The weather is nice and hot, too.

• **JB** This is a great environment to work in. Everybody is really open and friendly; it's like being at home, really. There are so many little rooms you can go into to record, so you never get bored. It is never monotonous.

We've written some really wicked tracks. So far, I'm happiest with the fact that I came up with the rhythm on a song called 'Only Making Love'. I also wrote some of the verses, so that's cool. Tim Woodcock wrote the top line and Oritsé wrote a lot of the second verse.

No one expected us to be writing these songs, not our label or our management. But they had enough faith in us to give us the chance to try. They could have said, 'Sorry, guys, it's going to be too busy and there's too much in the diary.' Instead they

SERGEANT. JB
No No..
Commando JB...
is he wearing underwear
hmmm...?, MA!!

said, 'Go and spend a week at Metrophonic and let's see what happens.' Now we've got the opportunity to show that there is some promise and songwriting talent there, something we can develop.

I know we can do it. Writing is not a new thing for me. I've always had a love of words; English was one of my favourite subjects at school. Now I want to develop to a stage where I can write for any artist in the world. That's my ambition.

• **ORITSÉ** I like recording in the countryside. It's pretty isolated and there's nobody around, so we can focus and get down to business. But it doesn't matter where I write: I'm happy working in my bedroom, on the road or before a show. I used to get told off at secondary school because I wrote songs during my exams and I'd be humming and tapping away at my desk. It really annoyed the teachers – 'What are you doing? You are wasting your life!'

• **ASTON** It's quite relaxing here, but I prefer the vibe of being at the studio in the city, where there are other artists around and you can look out of the window and watch people wandering past. I find that far more inspirational than being in the middle of nowhere. If you go for a break when you're at the London studio, something might happen – and then you can go back inside and write about it. But you can't go to the shop when you take a break out in the countryside because there's nothing but fields!

• **MARVIN** I'm so surprised and proud of how well we're doing with the songwriting. I wrote a couple of songs with the band I was in before, but this feels totally different. It's much more hands-on and the chemistry between the four of us and the songwriters is very strong. Part of the magic of JLS is that anything we do, we do it really well. We get the results. It's been the same with the songwriting. Although there are no guarantees that our songs will make it onto the album, I'm feeling pretty confident. We've done some really good work.

• **ASTON** I'm finding that writing songs evolves you not just as a writer, but also as a person. It's such a fun experience that it has made me want to write a lot more, so I'm busy expanding my vocabulary. Sometimes I come out with words and the boys look at me and ask, 'How do you know that word?' My phone is packed with short recordings of me singing two or three words. I'll watch a DVD and think, That's a nice name, or word, or phrase. When I go in the studio, I can share my ideas.

At first, out of all of us, JB was the most appreciative of being able to write songs. That was more his focus, whereas I was more interested in performing. Now he loves to perform as well as write, and I love to write as well as perform, so things have evened out. We're all loving every aspect of this job and discovering things we didn't know about before.

• **JB** We are really passionate about writing and the creative side of the industry. Like everything else we do, it is about making the most of our opportunities. People say, 'Why do you guys work so hard? It's always go, go, go!'

Well, as far as I'm concerned, this doesn't last forever, whatever anyone says. And even if it continues, it still has to change. We will get to the stage where we won't have the energy to work this hard. We won't *want* to have the energy because we'll hopefully have families or businesses to occupy us. Right now, we don't have anything that needs our immediate attention apart from our careers and so we are in a position to work hard. So we should go for it and write three songs in a day, or four songs in a day, if we can!

• **MARVIN** Most of the material is based on personal experience, especially experiences with girls. But with 'Private', we wrote it looking ahead to being famous and under scrutiny in the public eye. When you're famous, you have to be so protective when it comes to girlfriends.

• **JB** Aston and I wrote the verses of 'Private'. It is quite a simple song, but powerful, and it's a personal track for all of us. It's partly about how, as much as you come to terms with the fact that your own life isn't private anymore, it's hard for your friends, family or even your girlfriend to understand that their lives are no longer private either, just because they are your cousin, your sister, your mother or girlfriend.

• **MARVIN** We wanted to write something really special for our fans, without it being cheesy, and we sat down in the studio and came up with 'Close To You'. The chorus is: 'Travelling all around the world now/Seeing so many beautiful girls/But somehow no one ever comes close to you'. It's a really personal song, written for each and every one of our fans. We just want to say that, regardless of where we go or what we do, no one comes close to you.

• **ORITSÉ** It's a very special track. I wanted to write something for the JLS supporters because whenever I've been feeling down or something has happened and my mum hasn't been too well, our supporters have always made me smile. They give me confidence because they believe in me. They have helped me so much.

thursday 4 june

• **ASTON** We're coming to the end of recording for the album, although we'll probably do some more bits and pieces over the next couple of months. This six-week writing period has opened up a whole new world for me. It has definitely changed me and matured me.

At school I never wanted to go to English or Science because it was all about writing notes. I used to hate theory. I thought, If I get into the entertainment business, I won't have to do any note taking, I'll just be doing practical stuff. But now I always carry a pen around with me. I've got mashed-up notebooks shoved in bags and scraps of paper everywhere. I've even started reading more books, although I won't read in the car because it makes my eyes go funny.

You can write a song within a couple of hours if things are flowing easily. I find ballads easiest, because of everything I have been through. I once wrote a song that I showed to one of my ex girlfriends and she immediately knew what it was about. We didn't need to speak about it, because writing can be my way of talking about it. After that, it's done for me. It's my way of expressing something without having to sit down with someone.

Upbeat tracks can take a little bit longer because they're more complex. You have to take so many things into consideration with a song. Where do we want to start and finish? Do you want harmonies? What about the backing track? We've learnt that a song can be written in minutes or it may take days. We all have different strengths and weaknesses that we are working on.

• JB We all agree that it's easier to write ballads because they tend to be more heartfelt and so they flow more easily, but I don't want to be restricted just to ballads or upbeat songs. I want to be comfortable writing both. Yet it's very difficult to write an up-tempo song, especially if the sentiment doesn't have a real meaning for you. The best songwriters have the knowledge, insight and experience to know what fits and what emotions to bring out. They can say, 'OK, the song title is "Invincible" and I'm going to write a track that reflects that.'

Out of all the writers we've worked with, I think Wayne Hector is incredible. His talent stretches across the board. He is responsible for most of Westlife's number ones, but he's also had country hits in America, number ones for country stars. That says something. I'd really like to shadow Wayne and Ali Tennant, another great writer who used to be in the same group

MORE BROMANCE
NO LOVE FOR JB
☹

as Wayne. Just shadow them for a week and sit in on a session, whether it be here, in the States, in Germany or Scandinavia. Not to write with them, just to sit in the room and see what goes into writing the hook and how they get their ideas.

I'd like to think that there are no restrictions when it comes to writing songs. Later down the line, I don't want someone to say, 'Oh, he only writes pop music.' Because I like indie music as well, and a good song should be able to transcend the barriers between the different genres. Take 'Run', the Snow Patrol record that Leona Lewis recorded. It's a great song and it doesn't matter whether an indie artist covers it or someone does a dance remix of it. That's the difference between a good song and a hit song. It's also why there are so few hit songwriters. 'Falling' by Alicia Keys is another example – it transcends pop. That's my goal.

• **MARVIN** Our label has been great. They said, 'We're going to put you in the studio and if you come up with some really good songs, then they will make it onto the album.'

Between the four of us, we've written about 50 songs over the last six weeks. Often we've written two a day. We're really pleased with them and so are the label. I wonder how many will make it onto the album?

friday 5 june

• **ASTON** This afternoon, Marvin, my friend Chris and I were online at the Capital FM website looking at the list of artists who were going to appear at the Summertime Ball on Sunday: Akon, The Saturdays, Blue, Dizzee Rascal and even Lionel Richie were on the bill – and there's little old JLS!

Marvin said, 'Look at this poll!' People were being asked who they most wanted to see at the gig and 87 per cent wanted to see us, out of 15 acts, many of them worldwide acts. Akon had 1 per cent, as did Lionel Richie. Blue had 4 per cent and The Saturdays had 2 per cent. Unbelievable!

It's the first time I've had goose bumps since *The X Factor*. I felt physically sick. I was actually shaking as I looked at that screen. I couldn't believe that so many people wanted to come and see us. It didn't make any sense. We texted Oritsé and JB, and they were going crazy. Management tried to calm us down and told us we needed to take a deep breath.

sunday 7 june
Capital FM Summertime Ball,
Emirates Stadium

• **ASTON** When I woke up today I thought, I'll just take another look at that poll. Perhaps it wasn't a good idea – I was blown away by how many fans had voted. We were thoughtful as we got ready to leave for the gig. We were taken aback by it, spaced out. We all looked a little bit scared.

• **MARVIN** People like Enrique and Leona Lewis have scored 1 per cent in the poll. I just can't get my head around it!

• **ASTON** When we arrived at the stadium, we went into our dressing rooms, where we were told that we were singing two songs in the middle of the show. Feeling curious and wanting to see the crowd, we went to the left of the stage and peeked out. There were JLS hoodies everywhere. Someone saw us and screamed, 'JLS!' There is always one scream you can hear over the others and suddenly everybody's attention turned to us.

With all the faces and screams directed our way, a wave of energy swept over us and charged us up. Wow, this is unbelievable, I thought. Right, I'm ready to go on. Let's do it. After that, I was bouncing off the walls and running around enjoying myself. We lost our sense of disbelief and remembered why we were there and how much we wanted to get out and perform. It made it even better for JB and me that it was at the Emirates Stadium, because we're Arsenal supporters.

• **ORITSÉ** We had to hide because we were causing a disturbance. We wanted to respect the other performers and not get in the way. So we were backstage, hyping each other up and saying, 'Can you believe it?'

• **ASTON** I was set to be the first one to walk out on stage at the start of 'Umbrella'. Just before we went on, we heard an eruption. The video screen out front was playing a clip of JLS and the crowd reaction made the stage shake. Wow!

Before we go on, we always say a little prayer together; we come together and lift each other's energy. Why am I shaking? I wondered. I love to perform. This isn't me, I don't do this.

Sound check with Chipmunk at the Hammersmith Apollo

Go on CHIPPY!

The others went off to the other side of the stage. The piano started up and it was my cue to walk out, but my mic didn't come on. I could hear everything in my in-ears, which are custom-fitted monitors that enable me to hear myself and the boys singing, while reducing the noise of the crowd. But the crowd couldn't hear anything. I remember throwing my hood back and that was it. Hands up, a wave of people. What a feeling, this is it! Playing to a stadium must become a regular thing for us! Thankfully, on the start of my vocal, the mic came on and I started into the song. And I loved every minute of it; we all did. We were supposed to keep straight faces, but we were all smiling – we couldn't help ourselves.

I think Beyoncé is right when she says you have an alter ego when you go onstage. She's named hers 'Sasha Fierce'. It's hard to express how it works: it's like, light on, light off.

My mum says, 'That's not you on stage! Even the way you smile and walk is different.' She's right. Like a lot of performers, I often don't remember being on stage because my alter ego takes over. There is another me there. It's always been like that when I've performed – there's even a different tone to my voice when I'm talking before the song starts. It's hard to explain how it works; I guess it's all just instinct and subconscious thought and action. Then, as soon as I'm off stage, I'm back to Aston, back to being normal again, jumping around and being hyper.

Backstage at the *X Factor* final

• **JB** The Summertime Ball was huge: 70,000 people! There was so much hype around it and the crowd was the loudest I've ever heard. My mum said it was ridiculous because at one point she couldn't hear us when we were singing.

The Emirates Stadium is where we kicked off our first *X Factor* audition, so it felt symbolic of our journey so far, of where we've come from and where we've got to. We had an amazing day, really cool. I remember thinking, There are all these people shouting at us and we've not even released a single yet. The response was incredible. I just soaked it up.

Was I nervous before I went on? I suppose I was, but I'm different to some other artists in that I don't get nervous every time I go on stage. I get nervous the first time, but not the second and third time, because by then it's familiar.

The first time I went on stage on the Lemar tour, I was nervous. After that I got into it and then I was cool for the rest of the tour. The first time we did the *X Factor* tour, it was a similar thing although to be fair, when we did the O2 date, I was really tense because all the international Sony reps were watching. There were so many people we had to impress from label or management that I couldn't help being intimidated.

I get butterflies when I'm nervous, but I manage to put myself in a mindset that means they always go when I get on stage. Waving at people is a good way to dispel nerves, I find, and it's nice for the people you are waving at to feel part of the show. You can't do it every two seconds, just because somebody has their hand out, but there are times when you can do it and should do it, because it's a great way to show the fans how much they mean to you. It's something you pick up over time. You also have to focus on yourself, because if you get too engrossed in what the audience is doing, your performance suffers.

• **MARVIN** I was definitely nervous – it was our first major gig! And it was scary performing 'Beat Again' for the first time. But those nerves are good nerves and when you get out there, they always disappear. Performing is the best thing in the world. The four of us as one; you can't beat it. We do what we do best on stage and it's the best part of our job. It's such a contrast with the boring stuff, like the meetings with lawyers and accountants.

• **ORITSÉ** We are in demand! It's amazing. People like us and want to see us. It's incredible for any performer to have that level of attention and adoration. For us – four best friends, brothers – it is the best feeling in the world to look out at a sea of people who are all singing the song we're performing and enjoying the band. I feed off the audience: the more they are into it, the more I get into it. The energy that the crowd gives out runs through your body like an electric shock and gives you shivers. All of a sudden, you can't believe that this is happening to you.

'Let's not get too lost in the crowd,' we told each other because there are times when one of us can get carried away. 'Let's make sure we still deliver a consistent performance and stay in sync. We have to remember that we are a four-piece, a band.'

RITSÉ & HIS BEST MATE!!

I have good nerves before I go on stage. I get butterflies in my stomach, shivers down my back and I breathe heavily. To calm myself down, I breathe in, hold the breath for five seconds and breathe out. We always do a prayer together, too. Then we go on stage and we smash it.

Today I danced harder than I've ever danced before. Bang, bang, bang, the moves were just coming out! I purposefully try to hold onto the moments when I've got that shiver down my spine, because afterwards you forget. The buzz is so huge that it's almost like it didn't happen. A smaller show is easier to remember because everything is more contained, whereas a major show is quite loose; there is energy flying everywhere.

The nerves come because I am conscious of wanting to give the best of me and my talents, of reaching out and touching the audience in some way. I don't want to go out there and be rubbish. I'm never satisfied with satisfactory – I want us to be great. I want us to go up there and give the best performance of our lives. Every performance has to be better than the last. Bono from U2 said it once and I truly believe it.

• **ASTON** It was fantastic. I just want to relive it!

saturday 20 june

• **MARVIN** We had a party for my nan today, my mum's mother. All our family and close friends were there; I went with the boys. I'm very close to my nan and always have been. Mum had to work when we were growing up and my nan looked after us, so I spent a lot of time with her. She was very hands-on, like a second mum. We used to watch musicals and Disney films together and sing along. She was definitely one of my inspirations and she has supported me since day one.

She used to love it when I sang all the Rat Pack songs by Frank Sinatra and Dean Martin, so today I sang her favourite songs. It made her very happy.

• **ORITSÉ** And the boys performed the Dean Martin song, 'Ain't That A Kick In The Head' for her, which she loved.

• **MARVIN** It is hard to see her in a wheelchair. She's a lot worse than the last time I saw her. She was diagnosed with cancer in January 2009, while I was on tour; the doctors told my mum and dad that she had weeks to live. I remember just not being able to take it in. It's hard to believe that somebody so close to you, somebody who has always been in your life, is really ill, especially as she looked really well. She has always been such a strong woman. None of the family could believe it and we all tried to fight it.

'I really want you to come and see us perform at the O2 in February,' I told her. I had the tickets printed out and took them to her. It gave her something to look forward to.

'I want to be there,' she said, and she was. She was standing up and cheering us at the O2.

The next big gig was at the Royal Albert Hall in April with Lemar. I did the same thing again: I printed off the tickets and took them to her. 'Make sure you look at these tickets every night before you go to bed, because I want you to come to the gig,' I said. And she made it there, too. I knew she would do everything she could to make it to these gigs, because she has always been my biggest fan. It's a crazy time for the band, but I've been trying to see her as much as possible.

• **ORITSÉ** Today brought me back to a time when my grandma was really ill. She went through more or less the same thing as Marvin's grandmother before she died, years ago. I was very close to my grandma, so I can understand what Marvin and his family are going through. I remember thinking that I didn't want to be on this planet anymore if my grandma died. These days, it means so much when people say, 'If your grandma were alive, she'd be so proud of you.'

saturday 11 july
Hamilton Race Course

• JB We're up in Scotland for a gig. *The X Factor* is being filmed in Glasgow, so a few of the researchers are coming to join us for a drink at our hotel later. It will be great to see them again. And JLS's first single is out at midnight tonight! iTunes is the place to be at 12am!

sunday 12 july

• **MARVIN** I downloaded 'Beat Again' last night – yes, buy your own song! There's quite a lot of pressure on us to do well, so there are nerves and apprehension in the air. I feel excited and anxious at the same time. We can tell that it's going to do well, but will it get to number one? Or will it be number two or number three?

The way our lives go, it will probably be number two; coming second again! We keep making a joke of it. Of course we want it to be a number one but there are no guarantees. We're up against 'I've Got A Feeling' by Black Eyed Peas, which came out last week and looks like it will be one of the biggest songs of the year. Will it stick around? We keep saying to each other, 'What will be, will be.'

• **JB** When I get home, I'm going to download at least three copies of the single and the b-side, the whole bundle. I think it will go to number one! We've put a lot of work into this release and we've timed it right, so I don't see why we wouldn't expect it to. If it doesn't make it, then so be it; we're not going to throw all our toys out of the pram. But if anybody else can go to number one, I don't see why we can't.

• **ASTON** Yeeeaaahhh! Be positive!

• **MARVIN** Hey, it's number one on iTunes already!

tuesday 14 july

• **MARVIN** We got the midweek charts today, while we were in the studios at Kiss FM just off Oxford Street in London. Jo at our label called and said, '"Beat Again" is going to be number one! It's going to be one of the biggest number ones of the year!' Apparently we sold about 60,000 copies on the first day. Our fans are amazing! Oritsé broke down and cried because he was so proud of us. It will be a huge achievement for us to debut at number one. It means everything. I can't wait to tell my nan!

• **ORITSÉ** Seeing our first single going straight to number one was a bit too much for me! I was overwhelmed. This moment in the group's history, in our lives, now has a stamp on it.

friday 17 july

• **MARVIN** My nan has died and the whole family is devastated. I feel so sorry for Mum and Dad, particularly. They have had a long six months. They both quit work and devoted their lives to my nan for the last three months, so it's been a very hard time. I want to support them as much as I can.

• **ASTON** Marvin is experiencing the highest high and the lowest low this week. I will never know what that feels like, but he is dealing with it really well. We told him: 'If you need to talk, we're here to listen.'

At T4 Stars of 2009, Earls Court

We are all very upset, because we were close to his nan and his family. We loved the fact she could come to the O2 and lived to see her grandson have a number one. I call her the miracle woman, because she wasn't technically meant to be alive all this time. The doctors said that she had days to live and the days turned into months, which is incredible.

• **ORITSÉ** Marvin has been so strong through his grandmother's illness. Obviously, if he needs to take time off during this difficult time, it's not a problem. But he says, 'No, she wouldn't want me to stop.' I have to commend him for that. Marvin's courage and bravery and consistency and determination are giving him the strength to get through. We are all so committed to continuing to make JLS happen.

• JB Marvin's mum said to me, 'Keep an eye on him,' but he seems to be coping fine, really. We have always had a policy in the group of supporting whoever needs carrying under special circumstances. We do things as a collective, as a group, because it makes us stronger. We told Marvin, 'If you need any help, we are always here.'

sunday 19 july
T4 on the Beach, Weston-Super-Mare

• **ORITSÉ** To be a performer was my only goal when I was young; I wanted it so badly, for so long. So it was incredible to find myself in a dressing room in the same corridor as so many amazing artists today, from Dizzee Rascal to Basement Jaxx. Once upon a time I would have been starstruck just walking down that corridor. Now I'm a member of one of the acts and I have the privilege of performing at this amazing show.

• **ASTON** It wasn't a stadium gig, but it may have well have been because you couldn't see the back of the crowd! The faces seemed to stretch on forever. It was raining and wet, and our friend Peter Andre slipped on stage, so everybody said, 'Aston can't flip on here.' We didn't pay any attention. We were just focused on the single and where it was going. We knew from the midweeks that it was holding tight at number one, but obviously you need to hear the official chart to be sure. Come on! Come on, we were thinking. We just wanted to get the performance over and hear the countdown.

• **ORITSÉ** It would have been special to me if the song had been in the Top 5, but to be honest, I would not have been satisfied. I always want the best and as JB always says, 'Start as you mean to go on.' I felt that applied to our music: start as number one, let's go on as number one. And we made it!

• **ASTON** The whole day was a blur. I remember having a look at the empty stage before anyone arrived; that was really mad. We thought, It can't be that big! But it was that big. It was crazy when we went up there. They only had to mention JLS and everybody went mad. It was amazing to get such a big reaction and feel so supported, but I don't remember the performance. My mind was elsewhere. I don't recall getting on the coach to go home, either. The only thing I remember is jumping on Marvin, JB and Oritsé after we had heard we were number one.

• **JB** We were on the bus when we got a call, first from Capital, and then from Radio 1, and they told us the good news. We went crazy on the phone. So much has happened since we got together two years ago; it's a brilliant achievement!

It has opened a door: even if we don't ever have another number one, we are a number-one act. That label is attached and that label can't be removed. Things are looking good. Someone told me it's the first number one debut by a band for a decade.

• **MARVIN** The vibe was wicked today, even though it wasn't the warmest of days. Back home we had a party for friends and family to celebrate our first-ever number one (but not the last, fingers crossed!). A couple of our neighbours came as well.

It was our first party at mine and Aston's flat: you'd think two young guys would have loads of parties, but there's never time! We each invited around 20 people and it was packed. Since we don't get a chance to see everyone as much as we used to, it was a good opportunity to tell people how much we appreciate their love and support. It was nice to see my dad dancing in the corner and I'm really glad Mum felt able to come along. Hopefully it took their minds off things, if only for a few hours.

Aston and I went to the supermarket last night and bought 50 bottles of champagne. Luckily it was buy one and get one free. We were thinking, Have we bought too much? Bought too little? You never plan these things right. But it turned out to be the perfect amount because by the end of the evening, there was just one bottle of champagne left. Everyone stayed until 4am.

• **ASTON** Everybody was waiting for us at home when we got back. I didn't think my mum and my friends and family from Peterborough were coming, but then they just walked through the door to surprise me! They were getting me back because I always surprise them when I have a day off and I drive up there to see them.

tuesday 21 july

• **ORITSÉ** Earlier today, I watched our performance at T4 on YouTube. The stage was oval-shaped, with two parts on either side, so we had to break up our routine and then come back and meet in the middle to do the rest of it. I went the wrong way; I think I was being a bit complacent. It was annoying to watch it. After I'd studied it several times, I headed to the gym and went over the moves so that I would never make that mistake again.

wednesday 22 july

• **ORITSÉ** Our manager Phil rang asking for our passport numbers today. 'Are you being serious? Are we really going to

LA?' I still couldn't believe it. It feels like everyone is winding us up. But they're not. We are actually going to LA to shoot the video for 'Everybody In Love'. It's incredible!

sunday 26 july

• **A**STON Two weeks officially at number one! Thank you so much to everybody who has bought the single.

• JB We had a number-one party in a club in central London and the girl I really fancy came along. It was the first time she has been out with us and we had a wicked time. She's absolutely lovely and I can't wait to see how it develops!

If anything does happen, I'd like to keep it low-key. Some girls are possessive of the boys in JLS. People have told me they've heard girls saying, 'I hope JB doesn't have a girlfriend because I want to marry him!' and I wouldn't want to upset them!

I think it's quite hard to have a relationship in the public eye, with everyone watching you and knowing about it. Whoever you are, you want it to be between the two of you, not the two of you and everybody else. It's all part and the parcel of the job, but it makes me wary of being too open about my relationships. So far, I haven't been linked with anyone. I'm rarely in the paper, so it's all good. I keep a low profile and the focus is more on Aston and Marvin.

Sitting on the dock of the bay!

• **O**RITSÉ I've had quite a few difficult experiences. Paparazzi have chased me when I've been out to eat with a female friend and then I've seen stories in the paper, saying we are together. It's not so bad for me, but when the other person has a long-term partner, it's not a great scenario. I'm going to cope with it all by staying single. All the boys used to have girlfriends before *The X Factor* and I was the only one who didn't. My life was occupied by music and university, so I wasn't really interested in a girlfriend, although I always thought it would be nice to have one. I started seeing somebody when I came out of *The X Factor* but there just wasn't enough time to take it anywhere. My schedule is so full that it wouldn't be fair to have a girlfriend, although we all really want one. My girlfriend at the moment is my guitar.

• JB There are times when I read the paper and I make a judgment call on the back of it. Then I think, Actually, maybe it's not true, because I've read so many untrue things about us. It is just a natural reaction to believe what you read, especially if it says, 'a close friend said' or, 'an expert said'. You think to yourself, Oh it must be true, then.

I don't like it, but there isn't much you can do, although it's not fun when they say we've spent £10,000 in a club one night. Aston fell out with his mum over that story for a couple of days, which isn't cool, especially since it's not true. If it were true, at least there would be some grounds for them falling out, but it was about nothing. Luckily, it was only for a short time.

• ASTON When you first see untrue things in the paper, you get a little pissed off. Then you think, Don't be stupid! It's forgotten about next week. The first big story about me came from my ex girlfriend, which totally surprised me. It was a story on how the girlfriend before her was always trying to get involved and get back into the mix.

When I saw it I felt physically sick. How could she do it? She later told me that she hadn't wanted to, but I said, 'If you didn't want to do it, you wouldn't have done it.' It was a kick in the face. Fortunately, I have a lot of friends who know me from back in the day and they would never say anything to the press. We are all tight.

• ORITSÉ I don't really read magazines or papers very often, but when I do see something untrue about me, I usually just say, 'Whatever!' But one piece I saw did really get to me – it described me flirting with every girl in the room while I was seeing another girl. I hated the thought of my mum reading it and thinking that I'd play around with people's feelings like that, because I wouldn't. I treat people how I want to be treated myself. So much of what you read is not true.

I have a totally different perspective when I read newspapers these days. Still, I'm glad they talk about me because it means I'm relevant. It's better to be talked about, than not talked about, to paraphrase Oscar Wilde.

wednesday 29 july
In the studio, West Kensington

• **ORITSÉ** Today we recorded a song called 'Heal This Heartbreak'. When we wrote it, I was thinking about a girl who brushed me off when I was 15, so it's quite a deep song for me. I was drawing on that life experience and I was almost scared to expose it, but I didn't stop my flow; I allowed the stream to keep running. I think people receive music best when you are absolutely honest and this felt like a true reflection of what I went through at that time. It was good, because it helped me get over it once and for all.

saturday 1 august
Heathrow to LAX

• **MARVIN** Went out clubbing with the boys last night and didn't get home until 5am. Why did we think it would be a good idea to have a big night before we flew to Los Angeles? Our excuse is that 'Beat Again' is still number one, but I didn't much feel like celebrating this morning. I was supposed to get up at 7am to go to the airport, but I slept through my alarm clock and at 8am Aston was banging on my door, shouting, 'Marv, we have got to go! Come on!'

'Don't worry about it,' I mumbled deliriously, sleep talking; I had no idea what I was saying.

A couple of minutes later, I woke up with a start and realised that our flight to LA was at 9.40am. Luckily I'd packed my bag before we went out last night, so I made a quick exit from my bed, threw on some random clothes, made it to the front door in a record two minutes and jumped in the car that was waiting outside. The driver was brilliant. He got us from home to the airport in 20 minutes, when it usually takes 45 minutes at least. We were panicking all the way, thinking we were going to miss our flight. Luckily we made it just in time and got to Heathrow an hour before the flight left. Won't do that again!

I'm showing Ritsé how to rap!!! None... and i mean NONE OF YOU CAN RAP!!! ...

We got on the plane and I went to sleep straightaway; we were flying in business and so we had beds, thankfully. Oritsé was lying next to me and we both fell asleep for a couple of hours. We woke up thinking that we were well on our way to LA, but then I looked out of the window and saw loads of British Airways planes. We were still at Heathrow; we hadn't even taken off! The plane was delayed for four hours on the ground before we even set off.

• **ORITSÉ** Marvin and I sat next to each other. We constantly played with the blind that divided our beds. He kept pulling it up, and I kept pulling it down; we wound each other up over this blind for most of the flight.

• **ASTON** I was so excited when we got on the plane. OK, it wasn't a holiday, but it was business class! I was a bit surprised when I was directed upstairs, because the other boys were sitting downstairs. 'What?' I said.

'Yes, you're upstairs,' the stewardess said. I went up there to find that there was a girl of around 19 or 20 in the bed next to mine, on the other side of the partition that divided us.

I went straight downstairs to tell the others. 'You are not going to believe the flight I'm going to have! Come upstairs.'

They all came up, one by one. 'It would happen to you, wouldn't it?' Oritsé and Marvin had to sit together and JB had to sit next to some bloke.

'Oh well, it happened to the best of us,' I joked. It was a funny flight.

When I finally sat down, I said to the girl, 'Hi, how are you doing?'

'Hello, how are you?'

Gradually, we got into conversation. 'Can you get the stewardess?' she asked.

'Yes, do you want a drink?' I asked.

One thing led to another. 'Just so you know, I think your music is great,' she said.

'Ah, thank you very much!'

It's weird spending so long with someone you don't know. She did a lot of talking, even when I was trying to watch a film. After nine-and-a-half hours together, I got off the flight knowing a lot about her, the kind of stuff that you usually only learn about someone over time. 'I know you now!' I said.

'Take my number,' she said. I took her number, but warned her that we probably wouldn't have any time off in LA.

sunday 2 august
Le Montrose Hotel, West Hollywood

• **ORITSÉ** Now we're in LA and suddenly nobody knows who we are. It's weird, because for the last few months we haven't even been able to go on public transport in England. Suddenly we're back to square one, back to life before *The X Factor*. It's a nice change, even though we miss our English fans. We can actually walk down Melrose and shop and drink shakes and eat food together. It's the first time we've been able to do that in ages.

• **MARVIN** In London, we can't go anywhere together. If all four of us tried to walk down Oxford Street, it would be chaos, with people wanting autographs and following us around. We wouldn't dream of doing it. Here it is completely different!

• **ASTON** It's weird to think that we were being mobbed in England a few days ago. Some English people have recognised us and shouted, 'JLS!', but no one else knows us.

• **JB** I like cities, but only when you can be anonymous. That's why I wouldn't like to live in the centre of London. Luckily, I can still get away with being anonymous if I'm not smack bang in the middle of the city. Around where I live, I can walk down the road and not be recognised or stopped, on the whole. It's the same here.

monday 3 august

• **ORITSÉ** The shoot was great. I have to admit that I kind of fell in love with my video girl. She's a model/actress and it was her first time doing a video. 'Pretend you haven't seen me in 10 years,' I said. 'This is the first time we are seeing each other after all that time. That's how real it has to be.'

She really got into it. We both did. While we were trying to get into the moment on set, a kiss happened. The directors started saying, 'Ooh!' and wolf-whistling and all sorts. Then it happened again. Everybody was like, 'OK, now calm down, guys. This is a video, not real life.'

When we finished shooting, she said, 'Don't leave it 10 years next time, please!'

She was amazing, but nothing materialised . . .

• **ASTON** We all left the video shoot totally in love! It was inevitable, because we got to pick our video partners, so we were already attracted to them straightaway. No matter what their personality was like, their look was already there.

Mine was an American actress called Tara. What was really odd was that she was exactly like me in every way: her personality, the jokes we laughed at and the banter. Obviously some wires were crossed because of the cultural barrier and I had to explain stuff to her, but she was always doing accents and funny voices, just like I do. 'You are exactly like him!' JB said. It was noticeable to everyone. She was my dream girl.

• JB I didn't want to get up today. I wanted to stay in bed, because I've got a really bad cold. Then I was late to the shoot, because I didn't realise that we were supposed to leave at 10am. I got up at 10.30am and realised my mistake. 'Oh no, I'm late for the video shoot!' I started to panic a little bit, but Tom from the label waited behind for me and I went with him.

I took a cold remedy that made me feel a bit better. My video girl Kirby knew I had a cold, but we're professionals and anyway I didn't do an Oritsé and kiss her! She was cool to work with. She came across as a little bit shy, perhaps because she hadn't had a main role in a video before, but we got on well.

I'm used to playing to the camera now; it's all about putting across your personality. My style today was purposefully quite conservative. I guess I am quite conservative, with a bit of a twist. Generally I'm the kind of person who gets straight to the point. Sometimes it's a bit too much, but I don't like beating around the bush. I'm not very flowery! I don't dress things up.

wednesday 5 august

• **MARVIN** I love LA! It feels like a holiday even though we're working, partly because the weather is just fantastic. We've done loads in the last few days, including a photo shoot with the guy who did all the *Entourage* photo shoots. Most of the shots were taken in the studio, but we did one set-up where we walked down one of the main LA boulevards in the middle of three lanes of traffic! In between shooting the video, we've been shopping on Melrose Avenue, Rodeo Drive and the Beverly Center.

• **ASTON** I keep saying, 'I just want to live here!' The vibe is so relaxed. Everyone walks around looking relaxed and cool . . .

Shooting the video for 'One Shot'

• **JB** This is my first time in LA. I've never had an urge to visit before, but it's a fantastic place. It's funny, because everything I know about LA comes from TV and films. The reality is different obviously, so it's nice to see it in the flesh. When you watch it on TV, it's all go go go, but it's not really like that. We went shopping one day, and the shops didn't open until 10.30am or 11am, which seemed kind of late. I'm sure that when they do have their events like the Oscars, it goes kind of crazy, like in London when we have the Brits, but right now it's very relaxed and cool.

I wouldn't have a problem holidaying here every year, or spending a portion of the year here, but I wouldn't live here permanently.

LA is cool but it's not like NYC or Paris, maybe because it is so spread out. I'd probably pick Paris out as somewhere I'd like to live; Paris is beautiful, especially around the Sacré Cœur. I used to go to France two or three times a year as part of an exchange programme at school, so I've been there quite a few times. But here I am dreaming of Paris when I'm in LA … it's mad! It's time to have a shower, because we're going out tonight

• **ASTON** The food is great here. JB and I are always saying – in fact, we all say it – that when someone's making food, they should make it with love. In LA, they love to cook. They love to make food. And even though I'm not the biggest guy in the world, I love to eat.

In LA they serve the kind of portions I want for a meal. You order ribs in London and you get four or five. Here it's totally different! Last night we went out to eat and, stupid enough, we wanted a starter, a main and a dessert. 'Some ribs and side fries for my starter, please,' I told the waitress.

'Ribs for your starter?' she said. 'Are you going to eat that on your own?'

'Yes, that's fine. It's all good.'

But when she brought it over, I thought, Oh dear! Normally, I am very reluctant to give out any ribs when we go to a Chinese in London. JB is the same. We're both possessive about our ribs. But last night we were saying to the others, 'Do you want to try some ribs? Have a rib! Have two. It's fine.' I'd also ordered a burger afterwards and the burger was giant, so I totally overate!

• **MARVIN** We had a reality check trying to get into a club tonight. Nobody knew who the hell we were; we were just four guys trying to get into a night club. 'Sorry guys, you are not coming in,' the bouncer said firmly.

Big STRONG MARV

'Look, we are over from the UK and we need to get in there! All of our people are in there,' we kept telling him.

Twenty minutes later, we still hadn't got anywhere. By now the guys on the door were being really rude to us. 'Guys, can you move away from here,' they said. 'There is no way you are coming in here tonight. Just move on.'

Eventually our friend who was looking after us in LA managed to get us in. I couldn't help glaring at the guy on the door as I passed him because he had wound us up so much.

Inside the club, there was another reality check in store. Wherever we go in London, we get a lot of attention from girls, but when a girl in the club walked past me and I tried to take her by the hand to talk to her, she pulled away from me, looked me up and down witheringly and said, 'I don't think so!'

Oh man, this is definitely bringing us back down to earth, I thought. It was funny. In London, most girls would have given me more than the time of day. Over here, they don't know us or care.

• **ASTON** I've forgotten how to talk to women! In London I've become used to having the back-up confidence of being in my comfort zone. There's always the worry that someone is only going to like you because you're in JLS, but in general you can just go up to a girl if you want to. But I've forgotten what to do when I'm out of my comfort zone. What do I say? Do I say hello? I haven't done it for so long. The only girls I've got chatting to here are English, because it's easier to know what to say to them.

When we finally got into the club, I was still getting hit by jet lag, so I just danced all night. A couple of girls walked by and said, 'Oh my God, you are from England!' I didn't know what to say next, so I just said, 'Lovely to meet you. Bye!'

When we get home, we'll really appreciate the attention again. Normally we don't have to organise anything when we go out. We can walk into any club in London now, wearing trainers, a T-shirt, jeans, with paps everywhere, and it's fine.

I take my time getting to a club now. I don't want to get there early, because if I do, some people won't be allowed in, because they don't want it too packed for JLS. I feel bad about that, so I say, 'We'll get there for 11pm or midnight – or later.' It's fine, because we know we're going to get in. The London clubs love to look after us.

That's what you call a High Top!! hehe...

• **MARVIN** We are in a bit of a Catch-22 situation with women, though. When we go out in London, we get a lot of attention, but it doesn't really interest us. We know that some girls are only throwing themselves at us for one reason: they know who we are and they think we have money, success and fame. You have to be wary of those girls. You have to worry about them selling stories, kiss and tells. We love what we do and of course people are attracted to us because of it, but we have to question the motives of every single person who comes into our life, whether they're male or female.

The other side of the story is that the decent girls, the ones you would take home to your mum, are not interested in us, because they think that we go with all these girls who throw themselves at us. They think you are a ladies' man and sleeping with all these women. You have to try and prove to them that you are not. It's hard finding the balance. I really want a girlfriend and it's difficult to find a girl who will understand the job I do and trust me.

• **ASTON** Before JLS, I was always in a relationship. I love to be in a relationship. I was never really single, but I've had to learn how to be single now. I miss being in a relationship, yet at the same time I don't miss it. It's nice not having to call and constantly text someone. When you are single, you only get in touch with someone when you really want to, not because you feel you should. But I also miss the closeness of being with someone I love.

thursday 6 august

• **ORITSÉ** A couple of people have said that you know you've made it when you go to LA to shoot a video. But I can't imagine ever feeling like I've made it. We're just at the beginning of this journey and hopefully we've still got a long way to go.

OK, you can feel you've made it when you are Paul McCartney and you've sold over a billion records. But I don't think Michael Jackson ever said he'd made it. Michael Jackson always thought there was more to life, and so do I. Once I've learned guitar, I'm going to learn drums and piano. There is always more to learn. We stay grounded because there is always more to do. There is so much more to achieve. The boys tease me and say they can see me as a one-man band with my guitar and my drum on my back . . .

friday 7 august
Heathrow Airport

• JB We're home! And we've got the weekend off! I'm just going to sleep and sleep . . .

tuesday 11 august

• MARVIN It was my nan's funeral today. The boys and all of my family were there.

• **ASTON** My mum and dad came down because they are close to Marvin's family now. It was the kind of funeral where you celebrate someone's life. Everyone was upset, but celebrating and laughing about times they remembered. In a weird way, it was a really nice day. We all shed a tear, but it's a comfort to think that Marvin's nan will be watching over him and all of us to make sure we are fine.

• **MARVIN** It has been a real comfort for me that my nan was alive when 'Beat Again' went to number one. She was so happy! She got to see me doing what she would have wanted me to do.

It's only now beginning to sink in how hard and strange the week was when she died. There I was with my career flying, having the best week of my life, sharing a fantastic time with my three best mates; things couldn't have been better. But in my personal life, I was losing one of the closest people to me. It was really tough, especially for my mum. Her son was having a fantastic week but she was also losing her mum.

saturday 29 august

• **ORITSÉ** We've been nominated for two MOBOs and I am in a state of shock!

In the Green Room, *Friday Night with Jonathan Ross*

Ever since I was a kid, I've watched the MOBO Awards. It's crazy to think that the founder of the MOBOs, Kanye King, came to my university two years ago and gave a talk about how she had put together the Awards; it's even crazier to think that after I watched the 2007 Awards, when Jamelia and Shaggy hosted, I went to see the boys and showed them notes about the Awards and people's performances on the show. 'Maybe we could get tickets one year to attend as a band,' I said, 'and we should think about competing for the MOBO Unsigned Award.' But instead, we're going as MOBO nominees!

I'm so excited. It's our first prestigious award nomination. But I want to perform on the show more than I want to win an award. It's a possibility and I hope it works out, because that would mean much more to me. I love the feeling of being on stage. I feel so alive: the whole universe and the whole world comes together in that moment. It's such a buzz. It feels like I'm addicted to it. Why? Maybe I'm just a show-off. Also, I love entertaining people. I'm always aware that I'm one of the lucky few people to get the opportunity to perform at major scale events and in major places.

• **Aston** Two MOBO nominations? I can't believe it. It's not sinking in. It doesn't make sense . . .

• JB Even though we've only released 'Beat Again', we were kind of hoping for one nomination. Then again, it is unheard of for a group to be recognised so early on, so we weren't sure if we were clutching at straws. If I'm honest, we really just wanted to go to the ceremony, because we all watched it when we were younger. So to be invited along and be nominated is just incredible. We're really pleased! It is amazing to be recognised by an organisation like the MOBOs.

wednesday 9 september
The Jonathan Ross Show

• **Marvin** Obviously we were nervous this evening because a lot of people watch *Friday Night with Jonathan Ross* and Jonathan is very quick and sharp. After the interview, we suggested singing something different, an indie song. 'Somebody Told Me' by the Killers worked well for four harmonies.

Before the show, Jonathan Ross told us that he has a perspex glass floor in his bedroom and he stores all his trainers and shoes under it. Like me, he is a big fan of Vivienne Westwood.

I've only started getting into fashion over the last year or two, since we started doing this, I suppose. And now we have a stylist, too. Vivienne Westwood and Alexander McQueen are my two favourite designers. Also a label called Unconditional, as well as All Saints and Diesel.

thursday 10 september
Book signing, Lakeside Shopping Centre

• **ORITSÉ** Our book, *JLS: Our Story So Far*, was published this week! We're really proud of it; I hope the fans like it. I'm really shocked by how many people have come out to see us at Lakeside! I don't think any of us were expecting this. It's incredible, insane. I can't believe how passionate all these girls are about us.

• **ASTON** It was very interesting – I think that's the word for it. The whole place was absolutely rammed with people who had come along to get their book signed. I've been shopping at Lakeside many times, but I've never seen it like that. It really was amazing.

I never get tired of writing signatures; I just do a big A and a scribble that looks like the rest of my name. The boys are always complaining and threatening to turn their signatures into a squiggle, but I'm fine. I'm the quickest at signing!

I'm the one with the fewest nicknames, too. The others call me 'Ast'. Oritsé has about 50 nicknames. We call him 'Glitzy Oritsy', 'Reesh', 'O' and 'Nightwalker'. We call JB 'J' or 'Jaybes'. I just call Marvin 'Marv'.

• **JB** Oritsé has a million nicknames – we call him everything under the sun. I call Marvin 'Desh', because he looks like the bad guy in *The Bourne Supremacy*. I call him 'Petrol' as well, because back in the day when we were UFO, before we changed our name to JLS, he was known as 'Diesel' because he's so efficient and energetic that it's as if he runs on diesel. I call Aston 'Boy Blue' because his colour is blue.

• **ORITSÉ** I've got loads of nicknames, but God knows why they call me 'Nightwalker!' I call Marvin 'Desh' and 'Oblong Head'. I don't have any for Aston or JB – I'm just always on at Marvin. We have that banter going.

tuesday 15 september
Live Lounge on Radio 1,
recorded at Aston and Marvin's house

Live in Marvin and Aston's apartment on the Jo Whiley show

• **MARVIN** It was Jo Whiley's last week and it was a great week, with Jay-Z, Kasabian, Dizzee Rascal, Biffy Clyro and us! I love that whole live style; it was wicked to be singing with just a cello, drums and a piano, even better to do it at mine and Aston's house, not the usual Radio 1 studios. We sang 'Beat Again', 'Umbrella' and a cover of a Lily Allen song; then we threw a little bit of Beyoncé's 'Halo' in there as well. I sang the lead on 'Halo'; the lyrics are quite fitting, all about chasing the dream and the fame.

Jo walked around the flat and went into my bedroom, talking about my trainers and how tidy my room was. How OCD it was the way I have my aftershaves and clothes lined up. I wasn't offended. I definitely like order – that's the way I am!

The only place I really feel myself is in my bedroom. It's the only place where I can shut the door and totally relax. Everywhere else, I am always on autopilot, with an element of work going on. Even when you are going out and enjoying yourself, you can never really let go because there are people watching you. So my bedroom is my haven.

• **ORITSÉ** It's really important as a pop act to show that you can sing live without any electronics and production behind you – just stripped-down instruments, voice and harmonies – and *Live Lounge* gave us the opportunity to show off our vocals. It's a legendary show and I really liked Jo Whiley!

We rehearsed intensely beforehand, but on the day I changed the flow of 'Beat Again' spontaneously. I always change my stuff, I go with the feeling. Our vocal coach had tears running down her cheeks while we were performing the Lily Allen number. For such an amazing vocalist to feel so emotionally touched was unbelievable.

• **ASTON** *Live Lounge*: we were just amazed to appear on it! It was one of the highlights of the year for me; I was in my element. I wanted to do something new with my voice, hit higher notes and take a risk, so I really went for it.

Sometimes, taking risks just happens. Since I rarely remember performances, I often watch something back and think, Oh, that was a new one! Today I sang a very high-pitched ad lib at the end of 'Beat Again'. How did I manage to pull it off? I'd never have tried it before, but it came naturally.

thursday 17 september

• **ASTON** Everyone keeps saying, 'We love what you did on *Live Lounge*!' Thanks, that is what we are aiming for! I think we seem a bit more credible now.

• JB You know, I'm not sure I like this word 'credibility'. Surely any act that has a long-term future has credibility? I'm talking from our perspective, not the outside perspective, and I see us as having a long-term future. Well, I definitely want us to have a long-term future!

Whether you are James Morrison, Alicia Keys or Britney Spears, being in this industry is hard work. You still have to tour, you still have to do the promotion. We know first-hand what that's like.

monday 21 september

• **ORITSÉ** JB and I got stuck in traffic on our way to see the NBA basketball at the O2. I parked up at London Bridge and coincidentally he was directly behind me. As I got out of my car, he got out of his. He'd had the same idea.

'Let's get on a train, quick,' I said. We ran to the platform, jumped on a train and hid in the corner. At North Greenwich station, we sprinted to the O2. Luckily nobody spotted us, because we could have been mobbed quite badly, even mugged. The media and newspapers make out that we've got much more money than we do and we've heard it's a street cred thing to mug somebody who is well known, so I guess we were putting ourselves at risk. Still, it felt perfectly safe at the time!

tuesday 22 september
The Paul O'Grady Show

• **ASTON** This was fun. It's one of those shows where anything can happen. Paul O'Grady can go wherever he wants to go. He can keep things at a 12 or 15, or take it up to an 18 certificate level. It's an amazing skill. Sometimes he doesn't hold back. We talked about family, music and JLS being sex symbols.

• **MARVIN** It's always tough when people ask what it's like to be a sex symbol. The answer is, I don't know! We like showing off our bodies, so if that makes us sex symbols, that's cool, we're happy. It's one of those things that comes with what we do and we just get on with it.

• **Aston** I've never really thought about it, to be honest. I love the attention – who wouldn't? You want attention if you want to show off what you can do. But being a sex symbol is something new for me, for all of us, I think. I was always the little cute one in school, so to be seen as a sex symbol now is weird. But it's all good. I'm not complaining!

• JB It's a bit weird to be called a sex symbol. I don't really look at myself like that! When I was younger it always used to perplex me to see the way boy bands were revered. Is it something about what we do that makes the fans react in the way they do? It's very flattering, but it's also surreal.

• **Oritsé** If I really am a sex symbol, I'll accept the title. And if there's a trophy, I'll take that too! I feel unbelievably flattered if it's true. I've never thought about it before.

• **Aston** Later in the show we played a game in which Marvin poured water down a pipe with holes in it. Oritsé, JB and I had to block up the holes so that the water would run through the pipe and fill up a tube. As the tube emptied into a bucket, a duck was supposed to rise. The winner was the first one to get enough water in the bucket to make the duck tip over the rim.

Oritsé, JB and I did everything we could to block up the pipe. We had our tongues on holes, our fingers on holes, even our foreheads. Then Marvin took the full bucket and poured it all over us. We were like, 'Thanks, Marvin!' The water had orange colour dye in it and afterwards it looked like we'd been covered in St Tropez fake tan!

sunday 27 september
GQ Man of the Year awards

With Diversity

Aston: 'Doo doo daooo !'
Marv : 'what camera
am i looking at ?('
ritsé : 'this kids hair
is bag.... its
tickling me '
J : " im tired...!'

• **ASTON** People think that awards ceremonies are all about meeting celebrities, but you never know who you're going to meet. It could be people from the music or fashion industries or the press, anyone. Designers come up and show you their portfolios, for instance.

Some people say, 'You guys are too nice.' But if you are friendly, people are friendly back. When we are together, we work the room. Yes, you're always saying, 'Hello, how are you doing? Nice to meet you.' It's not boring, though; it's work, but we enjoy it.

It's interesting meeting all these creative people and seeing people grafting from the bottom to the top in different fields of entertainment. I'd much rather be at an awards ceremony than stuck on the telephone in an office again. This is my job now and I'm very happy with it.

With Mel B in Hollywood

Oritsé's dream come true, look at that grin!!

the boys think they are funny

wednesday 30 september
The MOBO Awards, Glasgow

• **ASTON** It didn't sink in that we had been nominated for two MOBOs – and that we were performing at the MOBOs – until I was actually there, backstage with my MOBO pass, entering a dressing room that said 'JLS' on the door.

The first award we were nominated for was for Best Newcomer. There was a camera right on us as the winner was announced, which surely meant something. We were saying, 'Have we won? The camera is pointing at us. Oh my God. We've won!'

'Yes, the newcomer!' I yelled, jumping up from the table. My chair flew across the room and people behind us were like, 'Hey!' We went crazy with happiness, hugging each other and jumping up and down. This was the award we wanted, the one we were hoping for. It meant people were noticing our music.

• **MARVIN** It was the first award to be read out. We were up against Alexandra. We thought, There is no way we can lose again to Alex. Please, if there is any justice, we have to win something tonight. So it was great to win an accolade finally and of course it would have still been the same feeling if Alexandra hadn't been in the category. Just to be recognised as a winner was great.

• **ASTON** We had made a list of people we wanted to thank if we won – and for some reason I remembered all the names. JB was saying, 'We want to thank our managers … we want to thank…' His mind went blank, on a detour, so I covered my mouth and whispered the names to him. To be fair, he would probably have remembered them, but I helped him out anyway. Then it was time for us to perform. I haven't a clue what happened during that performance; I don't remember a thing, from start to finish. People told me that I nearly came off the edge of the stage at one point. 'Yes, but I was being careful,' I said, even though it was a complete blank. Everyone said, 'That was incredible; the audience really went mad screaming' – I don't remember that either!

We left the stage and were standing on the bottom of the stairs, where La Toya Jackson was rehearsing her bit. 'Hey, there are the JLS guys,' her manager said and she started waving at us, looking directly at me.

I looked behind me. 'Who is she waving at?' I said. I didn't wave back or anything. I came over all shy and scared. Oh dear, I'd better walk away, I thought. I don't know why I didn't just wave back.

There was no camera on us when the second award was announced. When they said, 'And the winner is . . . ' a cameraman filming at the next table suddenly spun himself around and flicked the camera on us as they said, 'JLS!'

This time we didn't jump around, because we were thinking, Best Song? Hold on, are you sure? That means our single is the best out of everyone's singles this year.

I didn't know what was going on after that. Walked to the stage. Think Marvin spoke; I don't remember. I must have looked lost, because I was totally bewildered. It was very surreal.

> • **MARVIN** I was genuinely shocked that we won two awards tonight! For a brand new act to walk away with two MOBO

Awards in their first year is insane. As if to emphasise that, Kanya King, the organiser, read out a letter I wrote to her not long after we started *The X Factor* at the boot camp stage. She must have kept it on file all this time! In the letter, I asked if we could go to the show and watch it. We didn't get a response at the time, but the following year we were there collecting two awards! It's a mark of how far we have come.

• JB I would have been upset to not have won Best Newcomer, but if we didn't win Best Song, then fair enough. There were so many songs in that category that we couldn't expect to get it. 'Number One' was a huge track for Tinchy Stryder and N-Dubz and I think 'Bonkers' by Dizzee Rascal, one of the biggest songs of the year, was also on the shortlist. I am totally amazed that we beat them.

• ASTON We partied hard at the after party, even though we had to be up really early for our flight from Glasgow back to London the next day. We hung out with all the other acts and artists and people behind the scenes. It was mad. You see everything.

At one point, La Toya Jackson told us to go upstairs and meet her. 'What?' It just seemed incredible. When we went up to talk to her, I didn't know what to say. I was lost for words. Now I'm not usually lost for words these days, but a Jackson? We all grew up listening to them and meeting La Toya felt like taking a step closer to Michael, my idol. I couldn't help thinking that, even though he has passed away, it's strange to think of Michael Jackson being gone. It's just so hard to imagine.

saturday 17 october

• ASTON We had dinner with Theo Paphitis, one of the guys from *Dragons' Den*, at a family dinner with his two daughters and their friends, his wife, his PA, Duncan Bannatyne and his kids. It was just a free-for-all! 'Let's go and have dinner with JLS!' It was kind of cool, although I had never really watched *Dragons' Den*, because we always love meeting our fans. Whether our paths will cross with Theo's, business-wise, we don't know. It's possible, although at the moment, we are quite comfortable coming up with the ideas right now, with our manager's input.

thursday 29 october

Christmas Lights switch-on at the Trafford
Centre, Manchester

• **ORITSÉ** If I haven't felt famous at any other moment, I felt famous today! It was crazy. The Trafford Centre didn't feel like a mall. I thought we were at a concert or something. There were thousands of kids there, all screaming. I will never forget the feeling of knowing that all those people were there for us.

    • **ASTON** It sounds insignificant until you see it for yourself, but wherever I looked there were people, people, people, all in JLS hoodies. As I stepped out of the car, the sound hit me. I could pick out odd little words, but mainly it was just a huge mass scream. It amazes me, because I've never screamed in my life.

        • **MARVIN** I have never seen so many people sandwiched into one place in my entire life! I think there must have been about 12,000 people inside the Centre and they were all there for us. I went on stage thinking, Is this really all for us? The screams for JLS were the loudest I've ever heard. It seemed quite weird!

There was a narrow staircase leading to the tiny backstage area. I was worried about people's safety. Everywhere I looked, I saw people squashed together like sardines. The kids were going

Female JLS!!

crazy, screaming and fainting. It took me back to when I saw Michael Jackson at the age of 12. I was probably screaming then, but the JLS fans are something else. I love them to bits! I've never heard anything like it.

When we left, it was like being a proper pop star. As we ran out of the building, we were chased by hundreds and hundreds of girls. Our security guys, Graham and Adam, couldn't believe it. Our radio plugger, Bob Herman, who has been in the industry for 30 years and looked after Take That, Bros, East 17 and Blue, said that he had never ever seen anything like it before. He was running with us, because the girls were so close behind us that the situation could easily have turned into a problem for us. If one of us had tripped over, they would have been on top of us.

After tonight, I think our security will be stepped up and I don't think we can do any more free gigs. When it's a free appearance, it's much harder to control because you don't know how many people will turn up. Things need to be more monitored, or something bad could happen.

We love the hysteria and the excitement, but you have to take into account people's safety.

sunday 1 november
The X Factor: The Homecoming!

• **ORITSÉ** This was really strange. When I walked through the studio gates, I instinctively headed for the contestants' dressing rooms. Then somebody said, 'You're going to the wrong place. Go to the Winnebagos.'

'We're in a Winnebago? Mariah Carey was in a Winnebago last year!'

'Well, that's where you guys are now.'

Then I remembered that we weren't there as contestants but as artists.

In the Winnebago, we joked about, shot-gunning for the bed to see who could get there first. Then I went to see the contestants: John and Edward, Ollie, Joe and the others. It was a great vibe. Some of the contestants were looking at us in awe, as though we were established artists, which felt a bit weird, but also amazing. I just don't see what other people see. It's taking me a long time to feel famous. I'm still trying to take public transport – the other guys in the group stopped long ago. 'Oritsé, you can't get on buses or trains anymore. People will know who you are.'

Someone looking in from the outside might say, 'You're a celebrity.' But I feel like an ordinary person, an everyday person. I have a job that I really love and enjoy and then I go home. I embrace everything that happens on the outside; I just don't let it get to my head or take over. On the inside, I feel the same as always.

Oritsé & Aston's "Girlfriend"! Ha Ha Ha

• **MARVIN** It felt weird to go back to *The X Factor* because it's the place that gave birth to JLS; it's where we grew and came into our own. Stepping back into that arena is surreal; we used to feel part of the furniture there, so to go back as performers was amazing. The studio audience gave us a standing ovation! I was quite nervous before the performance, partly because the *X Factor* audience is massive, but also going onto that stage brings back a lot of memories. After the performance, we were waiting for Simon to give us his opinion!

Aston said he would happily do it all again, from the audition to the final! Not me. I'm not saying that I didn't enjoy doing *The X Factor* – I loved it – but I don't think I'd want to put myself through it again. For the three months that you are on the show, there is so much pressure on you. It's incredibly intense.

• **ASTON** It was fun being back. I was very happy to be there and felt relaxed because everything was so familiar. We had performed on that stage 13 or 14 times before; we were used to it and that sense of pressure that we had the first time wasn't there. I treated it like any other performance and as usual, I had to watch it back afterwards to see how it went!

It was great being able to walk around backstage and go into the canteen, because when we were on the show, the acts never used to walk around. We went to see all the people we knew backstage and met the new people and the contestants. I did a lot of daydreaming and reminiscing.

• JB It was like being back at home: we weren't being judged, there was no pressure and we were welcomed with open arms. We were just there to perform and be ourselves. Everybody was happy to see us and it was great for us to see everybody. It was so nice to get back in touch with the people who had more or less run our lives for three months!

tuesday 3 november

• **MARVIN** Just heard that that our album is being released the same week as Robbie Williams' album. So there's no way it's going to number one. How can we compete with Robbie Williams, the biggest pop icon of the nineties? Still, it's great that we're actually releasing an album. Nine of the songs we wrote made the final cut, so we have so much to be proud of.

• JB I don't know of any boy band who have written so much of their debut album. It's incredible! We have just signed a publishing deal, which is great because it gives us a way to continue writing without necessarily having to go into the studio with a writer to pen something or get an idea down. We can just pop into our publisher's studio instead. Nobody needs to know. 'Guys are you free tonight?' Done. Simple. We can write for JLS or other artists.

When an artist records a song, a publishing company will buy the rights to the song for a period of time. The company pays an advance, which the artist pays back as the song earns money. Off the back of that, the company helps to collect the money the song makes, as well as helping to put the artist in touch with people who might buy the song to play on airlines and adverts. It's quite a complicated system, but I asked our lawyer to explain it to me and now I understand it!

That MARVIN "smoulder" is Contagious... haha!

wednesday 4 november
Blue Peter studios, London

• **ASTON** *Blue Peter* was a big thing throughout my childhood. I watched it on the nights I was having dinner early so that I could go out and play football. I remember seeing the presenters swimming with whales, skiing, meeting music and sports stars and introducing people who came on the programme to help charities.

I was never one of those kids who wanted to go on *Blue Peter* and get a badge for making something. I wanted to go on there in years to come as a footballer or singer who would help to make a difference, as we did today. We're supporting the 'Send A Smile' campaign, which is raising money to fund life-changing operations for hundreds of children with cleft lips and palates in India. So I've fulfilled a childhood dream!

• **ORITSÉ** I was most excited out of all the boys to go on *Blue Peter*, because I've always wanted a *Blue Peter* badge. When they gave me my badge, I said, 'Hang on a minute! I haven't done anything. I want to make something out of a washing-up liquid bottle.' But I took it anyway, very aware that my little 12-year-old sister might be watching!

friday 6 november
Dublin HMV

• **MARVIN** We're in Ireland, where the fans are amazing. We sang 'Everybody In Love' on the *Late, Late Show* and then did a signing at HMV in Dundrum, just outside Dublin. The signing was crazy; some fans went a bit mad and did thousands of pounds worth of damage to the shop.

We left the building by the back entrance but that didn't fool anyone. A flood of people immediately streamed around the back, looking for us. As we got into our mini van, two or three hundred kids surrounded us, banging really hard on the doors and windows, at the front, back and on both sides. That was pretty full-on and intense! It was scary: it felt like they were actually going to break the windows.

I was thinking, If this goes wrong, we could be in trouble. We were stuck; the van couldn't go anywhere because there was a road-block and traffic everywhere, so at one point I thought we would just have to get out and run.

• **ASTON** The Irish fans were like bulls in a CD shop! They were knocking things over, destroying things, going mad. But when they actually got to meet us, they mostly just stood there, shaking and crying, whispering, 'Oh my God!' They don't seem to be able to control the volume of their voices. They either speak really quietly or scream, 'I love you!'

'Hi, are you all right?'

'Can you sign this? Can you sign my face, my arm? I'm never going to wash again! If you sign my arm, I'll get a tattoo done over it.'

I was loving it when the fans were rocking the van; I was laughing my head off and yelling, 'Yahoo!' There were four security guys around the van, cars bumper to bumper in traffic, girls banging on the windows and getting pushed back, girls standing in front of cars and climbing over cars; everyone was ducking and diving. They were causing a riot, not caring whether cars were coming towards them. This went on for half an hour as we crawled a hundred yards down a little street.

I don't get scared for myself, but I get scared for the fans. They only see what is straight in front of them. They have tunnel vision and it is JLS vision.

• **ORITSÉ** They were running at us like Rottweilers to meat and the bouncers just couldn't stop them. They didn't seem to care about getting hurt, but I was very concerned. I didn't want the vehicle to run over anyone's foot or anything. I see all the young female fans like little sisters. I felt a lot of brotherly concern.

• **ASTON** It's good fun going clubbing here. Graham, our security guy, is from Dublin and he knows the hotspots. So we were very well looked after. Great! Thumbs up to the Irish fans!

saturday 7 november
G-A-Y, London

• **ORITSÉ** Just before we went on stage, we found out that 'Everybody In Love' is at number one. It's so amazing. We gave the performance of our lives.

Louis Walsh surprised us – he was secretly watching our performance! Afterwards he came up and said, 'Well done, boys! That was a fantastic performance.' It was nice for us. I always thank him for all he has done for us. 'It wasn't me, it was you!' he says.

• **ASTON** 'Everybody In Love' is number one! Things are just getting better all the time. Tonight was funny. We played up to the audience, getting close to the crowd and letting people grab us. During the performance, we ripped our vests off! The fans went mad. At the end of it, they gave us a cake.

I don't mind being a gay icon. It's very flattering, probably the most flattering thing of all. Fair enough, you can have loads of women fancying you, but you're definitely doing something right when both sexes fancy you!

monday 9 november

• JB *JLS*, our album, is released today. Now that is very, very exciting!

tuesday 10 november

• **MARVIN** The album is selling incredibly well! It's no surprise that Robbie is ahead of us, but it's only by about 10,000 copies. Perhaps we could overtake him? Aaaaaaaaaah!

wednesday 11 november

• **MARVIN** Robbie is now 6,000 ahead of us – we're slowly catching up!

thursday 12 november

• **MARVIN** Robbie's record company has reduced the price of his CD to £6.99, so that's going to give him a huge push. I can't believe we're so close, though – neck and neck! He's about 1,000 ahead, I think.

Thinks he's Mike's doesn't he???

friday 13 november

• **ORITSÉ** When you come out of a show like *The X Factor*, most people presume that if you do get signed, you won't have a say in how the album is created. So I think people have been surprised by what we've done. Until now, they couldn't put their finger on what JLS was exactly, because they only saw us performing covers of 'Umbrella' and 'The Way You Make Me Feel' on the show.

Being encouraged to be part of the creative process meant that we had a major influence on the musical identity of our first album. For me, it was really important to put out an album that reflected the truth of the band and the act, so it was great that we had the opportunity to express ourselves and be true to ourselves. It is a very personal album.

saturday 14 november
Birmingham BRMB Christmas gig, Millennium Point

• **MARVIN** Now this felt dangerous. It was really strange, as it wasn't our gig, but a gig put on by BRMB radio station and Birmingham City Council. We were one of the acts, with the Sugababes, Tinchy Stryder, The Saturdays, Pixie Lott and Calvin Harris, among others, but it just so happened that we were opening the show at 2.30pm. It is rare for us to go on first and I remember a sea of people.

Marvin with Rochelle from The Saturdays

The love is ALIVE!

WOOOO....

The gig was outdoors and it was cold, yet a lot of people were fainting: girls were being pulled out of the crowd and over the barriers; I was alarmed to see an elderly woman at the front being pulled out.

It is not unusual for girls to faint at our gigs. Our tour manager has always said, 'It's going to happen. You are a boy band. Unless I pull you off the stage, just carry on.' You have to be professional and do your gig, but it felt weird to see so many people getting hurt.

As we were finishing, we knew something wasn't quite right. I think they anticipated a crowd of 5,000 people and 25,000 people turned up. The area was not equipped for that many people.

When we came off the stage the organisers paused the gig, because so many people were getting hurt. As a result, the fans realised that we were leaving and there was a stampede to get to our vehicle. A barrier collapsed and people were injured, which was terrible, but no one was seriously hurt, thank God. Again, it is all very exciting, but the last thing you want is for people to get hurt. It was another lucky escape.

• **ORITSÉ** If something goes wrong at an event, everybody blames us, even when it's not our fault. Their theory was that if we went on last, we wouldn't be able to get out of the building. So I suppose you can't win. Crowd management is the answer.

• **MARVIN** Our album sales and Robbie's are so close that it's too close to call! Going out with the boys to try and distract myself…

Filming the 'One Shot' video

YMCA!!!

sunday 15 november

• **Marvin** This morning at 9.30am I had a call from Nick Raphael, our label boss. (I was still in bed, because the boys and I were out last night celebrating how well the album was doing.) Nick said that we had done it! We've beaten Robbie by 2,000 copies. We've sold something like 240,000 albums and we're going to be number one. I keep repeating this news to myself, but I don't know if it's sunk in yet.

We worked so hard and long on the album, so for it to go to number one, beating Robbie Williams, is just incredible. If it was the other way round and Robbie had beaten us by 2,000 copies, it still would have been incredible. The figures are amazing. The only other debut artist this year in this country to sell more records is Susan Boyle.

I couldn't help thinking of the list of goals we wrote in the *X Factor* house. We listed on paper everything that we wanted to achieve from the show. Every single night, before we went to bed, we'd read the list out and remember why we were there and what we were doing it for.

At the top of the list was to win *The X Factor* and to perform on stage with Westlife and Take That. But it also stretched ahead for the next 10 years and included people we wanted to work with in the future, including Michael Jackson, Justin Timberlake and Mariah Carey. There was an entry about what we wanted to achieve from the band individually, the type of people we wanted to meet, like the Prime Minister, and where we wanted to shoot our music videos. It pretty much covered everything.

One of the goals was for our album to go to number one, and now it has! I visualised the moment, thinking positively: 'It's going to happen, it's going to happen, it's going to happen!' And today I got the phone call!

• **ASTON** I was in bed, sleeping off my hangover from last night, when the text came through from Nick to say that we had beaten Robbie to number one. I ran out of my room into Marvin's room, screaming and shouting, 'We're number one!' That was quite funny. Then I rang my mum and told her, but of course it wasn't a surprise to her. '*I knew* you were going to make it,' she said.

All day I've been walking on air. It's all been a bit of a blur. We partied hard last night, at three or four different clubs! Ouch!

• **JB** I was also in my bed when Nick tried to call me; I wasn't impressed, because I was so tired. After last night, I was not in any mood to be woken up! So then he texted me the numbers: we've sold 239,643 copies and Robbie has sold about 2,000 less than that! The phone vibrated as the text came through, I looked at it and shouted, 'Yesssssssss!' Then I went back to sleep!

I was overjoyed all day. It would have been a kick in the teeth for me if Robbie had gone to number one. We love Robbie and we have so much respect for him and he's great, but because he'd been away for so long, it was gutting that he was coming back just as we were delivering our first offering. How many albums has he released? And this is our first one! I'm very competitive and I think that if we're going to release something, it should go to number one – not by rights, but because we would like to think it has the quality to do so.

J... what are you Doing?

Later, when I got up, Mum said, 'Congratulations!' and suggested opening a bottle of champagne. So I had a glass of champagne with my family at home and then we went out for dinner in the evening. My parents were really pleased, but they expect of me what I expect of myself and we have very high expectations in my family. My mum's always been a huge fan of what we do, but she's critical as well, because she wants us to be the best.

That's probably why I'm thinking, OK, so we've got a number one album now, but it's not the be-all and end-all. What else is there to achieve? We've still got another single to release and promote, we've got a tour that we're working towards, there's loads to look forward to. I don't want to stand still. There's a time when we can afford to relax and let things go, but at the stage we're at now, we've got to stay hungry or we lose. We have to do what the Timberlakes and Beyoncés have done, which is release number one album after number one album. When we become a household name, we can afford to say, 'Yeah, we can chill out and relax.' Until then, I don't want it to take me over, because then I'll lose perspective of everything else.

Another thing on our list of goals was that each single and album should have a cumulative increase in sales – so the next album has to sell more than 239,643 copies in the first week of sales! You have to set the goals high: we have to achieve more with the next CD, even if it's by only one copy.

> • **MARVIN** It's Mum's birthday, so this evening I went out to dinner with my mum, dad and brother. While I was sitting at the table, my phone rang. I never answer phone calls from private numbers because we get a lot of prank phone calls, but I was in a good mood and something told me to pick this call up.
>
> 'Hi Marvin, it's Robbie,' said the voice on the other end.

I immediately recognised the voice, but I still said, 'What? Robbie Williams?'

'Yes, I'm just phoning to say congratulations. You guys have done something incredible today.'

Taken aback, I walked into a quiet area of the restaurant. Robbie went on to tell me that he had released seven albums and every one had gone to number one, except this one. Obviously he was gutted, but he graciously said, 'You guys deserve your success.' He knew how hard we had worked. 'These are the moments that you live for,' he added. 'Enjoy them!' He invited us to his house when we next go to LA. He has a football pitch at his house! He also said to say happy birthday to my mum.

It was really humble and good of him to make that call. It was another big highlight of the year for me. If Robbie Williams had phoned me up two years ago, I probably would have been a nervous wreck, but now it felt like I was talking to one of my mates. He didn't have to do it. He was probably quite upset and annoyed with us, so it's nice that he phoned up to say well done.

• **ORITSÉ** I was staying in a hotel in central London when I got the call to say that we were at number one. I went into shock. I remember getting in a cab and looking out at people in the streets and just not being able to believe it. You don't know, I thought as I drove past. None of you guys have a clue.

I rang my mum and broke down, conscious of how much it meant to her. 'Oritsé, don't cry!' she said. But I couldn't help it, especially when I thought about how she was one of the few who believed in me.

'This band is going to work,' she always said. She told me that I could do anything I put my mind to and she encouraged me to have the confidence to go for my dream.

'Are you OK, son?' the driver asked. 'I can tell you are very special and you love your mum very much. Don't be upset.'

'I'm not upset. I'm just happy,' I said.

Just then we passed a huge billboard with the JLS poster on it. By now we were in Shepherd's Bush, the area of London where I grew up. I walked past that billboard every day when I was a kid, every single day for 15 years of my life, and now I was up there, with my three best friends, my brothers, on a poster advertising our album. That's me! I thought, in total disbelief.

Oritsé Wonder!!
watch out people...

We all called each other excitedly. There is nothing better than being part of a team and feeling a collective sense of achievement. It definitely wouldn't feel as good if there was only one of you. Sharing it with other people makes all the difference. In 20 or 30 years, I will be able to call Marvin, Aston or JB and say, 'Do you remember that moment? It was special.'

Later on, I drove back to Shepherd's Bush in the dark with my best friend, so that I could admire the poster without people seeing me. I feel so proud. I tell you, if anybody graffitis my face or draws on a moustache or a beard, I'm going to climb up a ladder and scrub it clean!

monday 16 november
O2 Arena, London

• **ORITSÉ** I was invited to Beyoncé's concert tonight! It was mad. When I went into the arena, loads of people started shouting and screaming for autographs. The O2 staff had to escort me out of the arena and I could only go back in once the lights went down and Beyoncé was on stage. I couldn't believe it. I was in a state of shock. To create that much hysteria individually just shows how much more magnified things are when we are together.

Eventually they put me in the sound booth. I looked sideways to see Jay-Z and Kanye West standing right beside me! Beyoncé's performance was very inspiring, because I could see the level at which she had worked on her creativity and her talent. Her vocal was incredible, her dancing incredible. She really touched me.

Afterwards I went to the after party with my brothers. A guy called Frank Gatson came over. 'How are you doing? You're Oritsé, aren't you?' he said. 'I'm Beyoncé's choreographer. I love "Everybody In Love" and "Beat Again".'

Its Spiderman ain't 'it ???

This is Beyoncé's choreographer! I was looking around me and thinking, Somebody is playing a prank on me!

'I'd like to introduce you to Beyoncé. She wants to see you,' he said. I honestly thought he was having me on, but I followed him anyway.

He took me into a closed-off VIP area and that's when I saw Beyoncé. 'This is Oritsé from JLS,' Frank said.

'Hi Oritsé!' she said. 'You guys are doing so well. You should be so proud of yourselves. I'm so thrilled for you. Just keep doing what you are doing.' Someone took a picture of us and she invited me to sit down at her table, but I didn't want to get in her way.

'Thanks, I don't want to take too much of your time,' I said. 'It was lovely to meet you. Hopefully I will see you again soon.' How amazing!

I met some other idols of mine when we went out to dinner with Boyz II Men! 'Are you being for real?' I asked our management when I heard that they wanted to meet us. It was mind-blowing; I've been studying them since I was a kid.

I was already at the table at Sketch when I saw them come in. I felt totally star-struck. As they sat down, they introduced themselves by name: 'Shawn Stockman, Nathan Morris and Wanya Morris.'

'I know who you guys are!' I said.

They gave us some good advice: 'Don't get caught up in the hype' and 'Don't get carried away with yourselves.' They talked about mistakes they had made and warned us against getting involved with the wrong kind of girls, because some girls in this game are only here to bring you down. They also advised that we keep our business to ourselves and not be too open; to be very careful with our money when we make it and to invest it; and to look after each other.

They said they were very proud of us. I said, 'You guys have inspired me since I was a little boy. Thank you for everything.'

Afterwards we went to a club and Wanya put his number in my phone. 'If you need any help, advice or support, just give me a call.' What? Wanya Morris from Boyz II Men!

friday 20 november
Children In Need, BBC studios, London

• **ASTON** When we finished performing, they said, 'We'll raise more money if you do some back flips.' I don't know what it is with back flips! Jonathan Ross loves me doing them, but I know a lot of people who can do them and better than me. Sometime soon I'll be going to the gym with some friends who are British gymnasts and they're going to teach me something new. They keep saying, 'You can't keep doing those back flips.'

• **MARVIN** We are having the time of our lives and so it's great to be able to return the favour. I'm an ambassador for the NSPCC, which is an amazing charity; I've always got a place in my heart for kids. We do a lot of work with charities, including hospital visits for children and other bits and pieces. We are in the fortunate position of being able to lift people's spirits when they are ill or feeling down. A couple of minutes spent by a hospital bed can make such a huge difference, so we try and do as much as we can. We're planning a concert for JB's charity, Rays of Sunshine, in December.

• JB Rays of Sunshine is similar to the Make-A-Wish Foundation, in that it's a charity that grants wishes, mainly to children who live with chronic illnesses, and some who are coping with terminal disease. For instance, there's one particular boy I met, who is really clever, just brilliant. He's got arthritis and he's had it since he was a baby.

He's in pain every single day, but because arthritis is not a life-threatening disease, it doesn't attract the attention and sympathy that other diseases do. So the charity helps children like him to fulfill their dreams – maybe to go to a premiere of a film or have a special day out. That's where the rays of sunshine come in. It's a really worthy cause and they've got a fantastic team of three full-time staff and 20 or 30 volunteers. One of the volunteers, Jane, basically works six days of the week for free! That kind of dedication is truly admirable.

• **ORITSÉ** I chose the Multiple Sclerosis Foundation as my special charity because my mother has MS. She encourages me to talk about her illness; she's happy if it helps someone else, so I'm always open about it. I'm really hoping that being involved will help raise awareness of MS. Ideally, I'd like to run the London Marathon next year for MS, but I've had problems with my knee because of all the dancing and movement I do. It's OK, but I have to pace myself at times, so I'm not sure I will be able to take part in a marathon.

I went to the MS Foundation in North London to see how it works and who does what. I met a young family there: a couple and their boys, who were 8 and 10, and big JLS fans. They were in shock when they saw me. They didn't know what to say, which was funny. Their mum has MS, so they were going through the same things that I went through when I was their age.

I was glad I had the chance to sit down with them. 'Whatever you're going through, it's alright to talk about it,' I said to them. 'You are very strong, both of you, and you're doing a really great job.' Their father became pretty emotional and broke down. He's been going through so much. Before I left, I did an interview for the Young Carer website, answering their questions and letting them know they are not alone, because I know what they're going through, and so do many other young carers.

• **ASTON** I remember seeing an anti-bullying campaign on *Blue Peter* featuring loads of sports personalities. It made a big impression on me and influenced me when it came to choosing my special charity, especially as I went through a little bit of bullying when I was younger. There's also the fact that I'm the oldest in my family and I feel protective of my siblings; I want to look after them and make sure they're safe. And that extends to younger people generally: people look up to us and I get a big brother feeling for them all.

• **MARVIN** Pixie Lott and Westlife were also performing on *Children In Need* tonight. It's great to be on the bill with some of these artists, but often you don't even see them backstage, to be honest. The only time you get to hang out with them is when you stay over in a city and happen to be in the same

Marv catching up with Pixie at Wembley......

hotel, as we were for the ChildLine gig in Dublin two days ago. We hung out with Taio Cruz, who has written some stuff with us; Westlife, who we know from performing with them on *The X Factor*; Louis Walsh, our mentor on *The X Factor*; and The Saturdays, who are great.

I've got a confession to make: I've always had a liking for Rochelle Wiseman from The Saturdays. I first met Rochelle when I was 20 years old and she was 16; I was in a band called VS; she was a presenter on a BBC programme called *Smile* and she interviewed me. I remember her being very mature and very good looking.

After that, I'd see her from time to time in a club or somewhere like that. It's kind of strange, because our friends were and are indirectly connected. Nothing ever happened though, because I had a girlfriend and she had a boyfriend. When she joined The Saturdays, I started seeing a lot more of her, because we were gigging on the same circuit. But she was in a relationship and seemed very happy. There was no getting in with her, even though I was single by then.

Now we're doing a lot more gigs together, we're getting closer and talking; JLS and The Saturdays often go to the same parties. There's a natural chemistry between us. There's nothing false about it. But she is still with her boyfriend, so I can't do or say anything! I will just have to forget her and focus on my work.

Tonight we met Terry Wogan for the first time! It is always great to hang out with people in the industry. The actor James Corden from *Gavin and Stacey* is the funniest guy I know and he loves coming out with us. On the music side, we spend quite a bit of time with Chipmunk. We often see people like Dizzee Rascal, Will Young and Alicia Dixon at album launches, too.

sunday 22 november
Dunk n' Funk Celebrity Basketball
Tournament, Brentwood, Essex

• **MARVIN** The whole place was full of JLS fans waving banners, cards, books and CDs and cheering us on. We absolutely buzz off the vibe they bring to events like this! It was a chance for the fans to have a bit more intimacy with us in terms of physical proximity, because usually they just see us on stage. It was great for them – and for us – to have that closeness for the day.

It was brilliant because we are all very competitive and love sport. We decided that we would only do it if we won and we went on to win the final 33 to 6 – a bit of a landslide victory! Thank you.

• **ORITSÉ** The best thing about being in a band is that you are a team, whether you are playing sports, singing, acting or making food. So we had an automatic advantage over everyone else playing against us, as we were already a team. I've been playing basketball since I was a kid, so I loved every minute of it. Plus, the fans gave me lots of birthday goodies ahead of this Friday!

• **ASTON** There were a couple of *Coronation Street* stars and actors from kids' drama series competing as well. I don't know how many back flips I did; it was just stupid. It kind of turned into a contest, with everyone trying to do them, so I kept flipping from one side of the hall to the other because I don't like to be outshone!

• **ORITSÉ** From victory to victory … I'm having an early night because we're up at the crack of dawn tomorrow for the 'One Shot' video. I'm really excited about working with Marty Kudelka. I admired his work and knew that I wanted to work with him even before I found out that he was Justin Timberlake's principal choreographer. Wow! Now we are raising the bar!

'One Shot' is a special track for me. When I sang my part in the studio, I felt really emotional and passionate; I gave my all. 'You only get one shot so make it count/You might never get this moment again.'

This is what it's all about, I thought. We have one shot at getting this single right, one shot at getting this album right and one shot at getting our career right. I wanted my vocal contribution to reflect that emotion and I can hear the passion in it when I listen back to it. I gave 100,000 per cent.

monday 23 november
Day 1: 'One Shot' video shoot,
Acton, London

• **ASTON** Today was awful. Dancing is my thing, but I kept getting it wrong. This is Justin Timberlake's choreographer and I'm getting it all wrong! This is what I've been working towards and I'm getting it wrong. Then two guys that do Chris Brown's choreography came in and I was still getting it wrong. They must be thinking this is a joke. Is it just because I'm tired?

• JB It was even more difficult for me than it was for Aston! Dancing is the hardest part for me, because it doesn't come very easily and I get frustrated. Plus, we're doing something we've never done before with someone we've never worked with before. Talk about being thrown in at the deep end! Still, we'll just have to get to grips with it and do the best we can. It's going to be worth it in the end.

• **ORITSÉ** We've been working in a new studio in front of fun house mirrors instead of proper mirrors. We couldn't see ourselves properly! We were really trying to work hard, but the way the mirrors distorted our reflections made it hard for us to learn the choreography. It was upsetting. In one pose we were really short and fat, and in the next tall and thin. Stupid. Impossible.

tuesday 24 november
Day 2: 'One Shot' video shoot, Acton, London

• **ASTON** Today wasn't so good, either. I didn't know what was going on. It's really worrying – it's just not going in. Nothing is computing properly. The eye-to-hand coordination just isn't happening. I think I need to sleep on it.

wednesday 25 november
Day 3: 'One Shot' video shoot, Acton, London

• **MARVIN** If someone had shown me the 'One Shot' video two years ago, when I was sitting in my office job in the City selling land abroad, and if they had said, 'This is what you are going to be doing in two years' time,' I would never have believed it.

As well as raising the bar in terms of the people working around us, we're constantly improving. We pick things up much quicker now, too. When we were rehearsing the 'Beat Again' video, it was such a big deal. 'Can we do this?' The 'One Shot' routine was a lot harder than the 'Beat Again' routine, yet we found it a lot easier. (Well, I did, anyway!) I've been shattered every night, but I love that feeling of knowing that I've done a hard day's work. We want to be tested all the time, so that we are always improving. We always want to feel that we are challenging ourselves, as it keeps us on our toes.

The standard has to keep rising because, looking into the future, our plan is to conquer the UK and cement our place as the number-one boy band. Then we want to release our second album next year and do another UK tour, an arena tour. But the big plan is to go international, be it Europe, Japan, Australia or America. Who knows where it will be, but to go international, the standard has to be international.

• **ASTON** I had a bit of sleep last night and today I knew it all! It was in there; I just needed to rest. Usually I'm good at picking stuff up, but I think I'd reached overload. Anyway, it came together in the end. I still could have been 50 per cent better, but it looks great.

"Master Mike" cutting 'Ritsé – fresh neeeow!!

• **ORITSÉ** You can see where Justin Timberlake got his dance style from; his image and swagger is all Marty Kudelka. I really want to be like him! During this shoot, Marty has shown me that I have more potential than I realise. He has taught me to dance in a totally different way. 'Don't be mad at the floor,' he said at one point. 'The floor's not mad at you.' I will never forget those words. It's like, chill, relax and feel the music. In the break times, I asked him to teach me little moves and he was always there to give a helping hand, with fantastic results. It was a dream come true to work with the Talauega Brothers, who directed the video. They were involved with teaching choreography to some of my biggest inspirations, such as Michael Jackson and Ginuwine. We each had to do different solo parts and when I did mine, Tony said, 'I really felt emotional when you were singing! Listen to me, and I never want you to forget this: real stars pull from real places. That's what you just did.'

'I was thinking of a girl and I really felt like I was in the moment,' I told him, referring to someone I was seeing recently. 'Having that one shot – when you take a girl's hand and she comes into your life – or it never, ever happening.'

'That totally makes sense to me,' he said. 'You have a lot more potential than you realise.' It was nice of him to say so!

friday 27 november

Oritsé's birthday

• **MARVIN** Yeah! We bought Oritsé a pair of Vivienne Westwood pirate boots for his birthday – he loves them!

• **ORITSÉ** We didn't get to celebrate because we were so busy rehearsing for the Jingle Bell Ball. Still, it was a nice birthday because of the fans. I received a card from the JLS Forum, along with a golden plate chain with the words, 'Oritsé you are an inspiration to all of us. Thank you for putting the band together. We love you. JLS fans.' I was really touched.

monday 30 november

Noel's Christmas Presents, Sky studios,

London

• **MARVIN** Today was really nice. We met three sisters: one of them had suffered from leukemia when she was a baby and her oldest sister was able to save her life by being a successful bone marrow donor. The sisters went for a makeover in London with Noel Edmonds and came home happy, thinking it was the end of their day, only to find us sitting in their front room, watching TV! They were overwhelmed, just as I would have been at their age if I'd come home to find my favourite pop band sitting in my front room. It must have been fantastic for them.

Our Surrogate Father!

All the time you hear, 'My daughter is in love with you.' Or, 'My son wants to be in your band.' You think, Oh, that's really nice. But when you see it, when you meet the kids and you see their reaction and how they look up to you, it's fantastic.

• **ORITSÉ** I gave the oldest sister one of my rings to give her strength. I know what it's like being an older sibling and having to look after younger ones. Sometimes people don't realise that you need a lot of love too. I just wanted to say to her, 'You did a good job. You did amazingly, you saved your sister's life. What an incredible thing to do.' It was fantastic spending the day with the girls and giving them such a big surprise. They were all pretty elated and the parents were just over the moon.

• **ASTON** The girls were in shock, in a good way. It was really nice that we could bring them that kind of joy. They have been through a lot, but they were smiling. All the neighbours came out. What a dream!

saturday 5 december
Capital's Jingle Bell Ball, O2 Arena, London

• **ORITSÉ** Tonight was fantastic. Apart from our performance, the highlight was seeing Ne-Yo on stage, as he's someone I've really looked up to in the industry in recent times. He does it all: he writes and performs hit songs, and sings and dances to a high level. It was like watching a superstar perform. I saw Janet Jackson as well. I didn't get the opportunity to meet any of the artists, but I really enjoyed myself. We're performing again tomorrow – the only act to appear on the Saturday and the Sunday. Yes!

• **MARVIN** It's just crazy to be getting the loudest cheers and screams when you're around all these huge, global stars. They have had massive success, but everybody was screaming for us the most. Some of the other performers must have been thinking, Who is this JLS band?

I still think to myself, Is this all a dream? Why is this happening to us?

• JB I love the O2 arena. The last time we were here, we were performing on the *X Factor* tour; now we're here for the Jingle Bell Ball and hopefully next December we're going to be back here as part of our own arena tour! It just gets better and better . . .

monday 7 december
JB's birthday

• MARVIN Last night we went to Whisky Mist to celebrate JB's birthday. His present is a pair of shoes from Christian Dior, but we haven't given them to him yet. He's going to love them!

Instead of a car we got JB something he loves... HA! A BOOK...

• JB It was very stressful at first last night, because I couldn't get all my people into the club. I'd already explained that I had about 20 people coming down and they told me I could have 30 or 40, but then it all changed. I didn't understand why they were messing about, but I got all my people in finally and ended up having a decent night.

Wow, I'm 23 today! Tomorrow or the next day I want to go to Gilgamesh in Camden with the boys. It's one of mine and Marvin's favourite restaurants and the food is fantastic. I'm going to have the chef's special fried rice, some sushi, edamame beans, some tempura, a couple of sushi rolls and maybe some duck – enough for 10 people, at least!

wednesday 9 december

• MARVIN We did a poll on the JLS website: the song we wrote for the fans, 'Close To You', is the fans' favourite song! It was going to be released as a single, but it's not now. We are only releasing three singles from this album, but had there been a fourth single, this would have been the one. We're looking forward to performing it on tour early next year and dedicating it to the fans.

saturday 12 december
The X Factor: the final Saturday,
ITV studios, London

• **Marvin** We're back at *The X Factor* to do a special end-of-series performance with Alexandra Burke, singing 'Bad Boys' and 'Everybody In Love'. It's really cool to be on the show again, especially with Alex. It feels like a fitting end to the year!

• **Oritsé** I became very hyped up and passionate during our performance with Alexandra and I let out a spontaneous vocal. If that magic hits me, I let it happen, so I went with the moment. Usually I sing, 'Put your hands up, up, love, up.' Instead I sang, 'Put your hands, up, up, everybody, love, yes, yeah.' Aston looked at me as if he couldn't believe it.

When I hit those high, strong notes, it got the boys and Alexandra excited. Everybody did their best after that. I was happy that I helped trigger a feeling in everyone. Wow, that was the biggest buzz!

I saw Simon Cowell in the corridor afterwards. 'Incredible. Incredible,' he said. Then he tapped my nose and said, 'Well done, kiddo.'

• **Marvin** It's been a good *X Factor* this year. I think Jedward brought something to the show, an element of fun, and they went out at the right time. Obviously they weren't the best singers in the competition. Ollie was my favourite throughout. Joe is the better singer, but I liked Ollie from the moment I saw him. I really feel for them both today – they must be exhausted. Being a group, we had it a bit easier because the focus was never all on one person; it must be much harder for solo artists.

• **ASTON** It was a very good *X Factor* this year, but also a very difficult *X Factor*, because it was so diverse. There wasn't one definite favourite; there were three. If Joe hadn't won, I'd like to have seen Stacey win. I thought she was lovely when I met her, really great. Towards the end, Ollie was just reaching his comfort zone, so I think the right three reached the final.

• **MARVIN** It's funny that people sometimes raise their eyebrows because we come from a show like *The X Factor*. But it's a huge part of the music industry now and hopefully it's time to recognise Leona Lewis' success – and Alexandra's and our success – for what it is. We work just as hard as any other music act.

sunday 13 december
The X Factor final

Aston with Ollie Murs

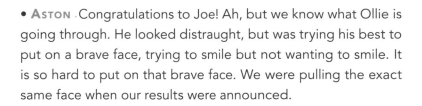
Will we ever win something?

• **ASTON** Congratulations to Joe! Ah, but we know what Ollie is going through. He looked distraught, but was trying his best to put on a brave face, trying to smile but not wanting to smile. It is so hard to put on that brave face. We were pulling the exact same face when our results were announced.

It feels like your world is tumbling down because you didn't win, and none of us enter competitions not to win. But Ollie doesn't realise what an incredible year he is about to have, if he wants it. In a way, I feel for him but I couldn't help laughing because he's got nothing to worry about. Watching the show tonight really brought it all back – and I wouldn't change anything at all.

monday 14 december

• **ORITSÉ** 5pm: I've just woken up! I've had 14 hours' sleep! Usually I sleep five hours, so that shows how shattered I am. All the lack of sleep has finally caught up with me.

8pm: The MOBO awards have arrived and I've just placed them up on a shelf in my flat, next to my BBC Switch Live Award for Outstanding Artist and my Dunk n Funk basketball trophy. I think I'll have to find somewhere else to put my favourite photo of the boys, taken at Hoar Cross Hall, a spa in the countryside. It was really cool there. We stayed in the royal suite, which was pretty amazing, and it was my treat, because I wanted to do something to say thank you to them.

tuesday 15 december
Plaque Attack

• **MARVIN** At a dinner last night with our record company and management, we each received plaques for our number one, 'Everybody In Love', plaques celebrating 400,000 copies sold of 'Beat Again' and plaques for the number one album, *JLS*, which has sold nearly 700,000 copies in four weeks. It's incredible!

Life has been mental and crazy since 'Beat Again' came out, it really has. We knew we were going to have an element of success, but it's hard to put into words how good this year has been. Let's just say it could not have gone any better. We're so lucky to have such devoted fans.

There is so much success around us at the moment. We've been the breakthrough act of the year. We've had a huge-selling album, which is the second-biggest selling album of the year, two number one singles and two MOBO Awards. And we're going to be performing at the BRIT Awards in February.

On the set of 'One Shot' video!!

This year could not have gone any better for a pop act. It is just incredible!

Someone sent me an article that quotes Rihanna saying that she fancies me. It's in the *Sun* today. One of my friends from back home saw it and said, 'You're really not living in the real world, are you?' It's true, I'm not. But it's still me, even though my life is crazy.

I feel very lucky. I've always loved being on the stage and I will never deny the fact that I enjoy the attention and the fame. I don't believe anybody who says they don't. There is very little downside to what we do. But because I've been on the same path before, I never, ever want to sit back and think we've made it. I know how quickly things can change and how fickle the industry is: how you can be hot today but not tomorrow. I don't think that will happen to us, because we've had a great start, but it's best not to be complacent.

• **ORITSÉ** If we can keep going for 10 years or more, I'd be more than happy! The key thing is that we understand the power of us four together. We've seen other bands make mistakes: nine times out of ten, going solo doesn't work. You have the lucky ones like Robbie Williams who break through, although he has had his problems; there are very few like Justin Timberlake. It didn't work for Gary Barlow, Mark Owen, Backstreet Boys or The Temptations. It didn't work for Boyz II Men and so many other people. Unless somebody has an incredible talent, like Michael Jackson from The Jackson 5, it's not going to happen. I used to want to be a solo artist, before the band, but now I can't imagine life on the road by myself. I don't think I'd enjoy it in the same way.

• **ASTON** The only problem is not seeing my family enough. But I've said to them, 'If I don't see you so much in the next five years, we'll make up for it afterwards.' See, I want to send them all on holiday and share the rewards. Fair enough, I might not always be able to go with them, but that's what I want to work hard for.

• **MARVIN** This week we're winding down for Christmas. We finish work on Friday, then we have two weeks off. I'm flying to Miami on Boxing Day, if British Airways don't strike … I can't wait!

• JB I haven't put my plaques up in my room because there just never seems to be time. My mum has the plaques I've given to her up in the living room so I can see them every day! I'll definitely have to put mine up when I'm settled in my own house and have a family of my own . . . At the moment, I still live in my family home in Croydon, right at the top of the house. My room's quite big and I've got the room next door now too, because I need more space for my clothes.

wednesday 23 december

• **MARVIN** Audi have loaned me an R8, my dream car, for five days! I've been driving my dad and my brother around. After such a busy year, it's fantastic to have some time off to roll around in this amazing machine. I was a bit nervous driving it at first, because it's a very powerful car and it's worth £100,000, but I'm used to it now. Being a four-wheel drive, it's been brilliant in this icy, snowy weather. Dad got stuck in the snow on the way back from shopping at Bluewater, but I didn't have a problem at all.

• JB Whenever we have time off, I've taken a car out for a test drive. So now I've test driven a Range Rover, a BMW from the 6 series, a Porsche Cayman, an Audi A4 and a Mercedes E class so far! I think I'm gonna have to go for the 6 series … I'm going to nickname it my 'sexy six!' Ha ha!

friday 25 december

• **MARVIN** Wow, Christmas! It's so great to be with my family, because I haven't seen a lot of them this year. My baby nephew Harvey is growing up so quickly!

• **ASTON** Christmas dinner was lovely. We did it a bit differently this year: we had Christmas dinner on Christmas Eve with just the immediate family – my mum, my dad and my brother and sister – and then on Christmas Day we went to my uncle's house. It was a nice and relaxing way of doing things.

• JB It's been a quiet Christmas with my mum, my brother and my old friend Daniel. We had chicken, ham, ribs and potatoes, rice, vegetables and salad and apple crumble for Christmas dinner. So we were well filled by the end of it!

tuesday 29 december

• **MARVIN** On Boxing Day I flew to Miami with a few of my friends. It was lovely and hot. We stayed in the Mondrian Hotel on South Beach for two nights and did a bit of shopping and a bit of partying. It was quite nice being somewhere where most people didn't know me.

The pool at the Mondrian is quite show-off and flashy, with girls walking around in bikinis. The sun was shining and everybody was in a good mood, so I was loving it. Then we bumped into Craig David, who has a place in Miami. I'd met him before in London and we spent a couple of hours with him, hanging out and catching up, which was great.

Then I flew to St Barts in the Caribbean. I know – amazing! One of the friends I was with is very wealthy and we travelled by private jet and helicopter, and stayed on a beautiful yacht.

the "smoulder" from "steve" NEVER fails...!!

It was really fantastic to be invited! What a surreal experience it was to be surrounded by millionaires and billionaires. When we flew to Saint Martin to get a helicopter to land on a boat, there was a queue for the helicopter and Eddie Murphy had gone just before us!

• **Aston** I didn't go away over Christmas, like the others did. I wanted to see all the friends I hadn't seen all year, rather than go away. First, I went home to Peterborough for four days, did the rounds, saw all the family and friends and ate loads of Mum's food. The best thing was having proper full-on breakfasts and sausage sandwiches, bacon sandwiches and fry-ups. All I usually have in the morning is cereal, because there's never time to cook.

Now I'm back in London. Loads of friends are staying at the flat. There's always someone around. It's fantastic.

friday 1 january 2010

One of Aston's
'intimate' moments...

• **Aston** I'm feeling fine today! Last night I went to a club in London with some friends. It was a lads' night. We went out pretty early, at about 7pm, and came back at 2am, tired and happy. First we went to eat at a local Thai restaurant, then we headed into central London. It was great in the club, but when it came to the run-up to the midnight countdown, I quickly got bored of the dramatic music they were playing. I wanted to get back to all the flirting and dancing.

So, about a minute into the song, but still a minute before midnight, I started shouting out, '10, 9, 8, 7 . . .'

Suddenly the lights came on and everybody joined in my early countdown, which meant that all the party poppers went off 50 seconds before New Year actually started. Whoops! Everybody was sending out their 'Happy New Year' texts at 11.59pm! My friends were literally on the floor, crying with laughter.

saturday 2 january

• JB Two days after Christmas I flew to New York to stay with my dad's brother. I came here to chill out and I've been sleeping a lot! People keep saying to me, 'You can't come to New York and sleep!' Well, I've been in bed by 10pm every night and up after 10am every morning, having 12 hours' sleep a night. Except for New Year's Eve, obviously, when we went out and had a late one. That was a bit messy. We had a great time. Oritsé organised it: for $100 there was a free bar and everything was sorted. We had our comedy 2010 specs on and all sorts. It was a good vibe and we danced all night.

There's a familiar sight ("this boy loves his pillow") WAKE UP!

It's my first time in New York, so I've been doing a few sightseeing trips, to Chinatown and Ground Zero and Little Italy. For my birthday, my mum gave me a helicopter ride over Manhattan and the Statue of Liberty, Liberty Island and Ellis Island. It was really cool. I went at 5.30pm and it was dark by the time we landed; Manhattan looked really beautiful lit up against the dark sky. The next day, my uncle's friend took us round Jersey and through Queens, so I got to see a bit more of New York than just Manhattan.

I also saw *Billy Elliot* on Broadway and went to see the New York Knicks play a basketball match. I really should have waited a couple of days and seen LeBron James and the Cleveland Cavaliers, but I was in a bit of rush. New York is cool. I'll definitely come again.

• ORITSÉ I spent Christmas with my mum's brother and his family in Canada. My uncle has lived in Canada all his life, but has travelled back and forth between Canada and England

backstage before our X-factor performance ... Nervous!

since I was a kid, so I know him and my cousins very well. They are very supportive of what I'm doing.

When I arrived at their house, I was told to take off my hat. 'But wearing a hat is part of my image in the UK. Everybody knows me from my hats,' I protested.

'Not in this house,' I was told. Back to real life! Back to being told what to do and having to obey and listen! My family don't treat me any differently to the way they have always treated me, which I really appreciate.

I was out there for a week, seeing my new baby cousins, being with the family and helping my uncle around the place. Our Christmas was very traditional: there was a tree, presents, dinner, family games and TV watching. I loved it.

A lot of my time was taken up giving performances to my Canadian relatives and their friends! My cousins kept saying, 'Oritsé is a member of a big boy band in the UK,' and so people kept asking me to sing for them. I ended up singing JLS songs wherever I went, which was a bit weird. I literally went through the whole album.

Now I'm in New York with a friend. It's cool, although people have been recognising me a bit more than in Canada, so we've had to be careful while we're walking around.

• **MARVIN** On New Year's Eve, I went to a party on St Barts. Gwen Stefani was performing; the guys from the Red Hot Chili Peppers were also there, along with other celebrities like Marc Jacobs, Jon Bon Jovi and the footballer Andriy Shevchenko. Later, I went to another party, where Beyoncé was performing. Jay-Z and Usher were there; we were all in the same area, drinking champagne and partying together! I had a fantastic time.

People knew who I was, but they didn't care. I was a small fish in a big pond. St Barts is a great island. People are really not bothered about celebrities out there. That's why many famous people go there to chill, because they don't get hassled.

My big news is that I spoke to Rochelle today. She has split up with her boyfriend! Apparently they've been having problems for a while. Does this mean I might have a chance with her? I wonder if it's too early to ask her out on a date? I don't want anyone else to snap her up. It's definitely time to get back to England...

wednesday 20 january

• **MARVIN** I've been pursuing Rochelle for dates, but she has just come out of a relationship and there's a lot to deal with. I don't want to put pressure on her . . . but I really want to take her out! It's so hard to be patient. I've liked her for such a long time now.

X Factor rehearsals
Really! How much WATER does
One band Need!!
ha!

• **ASTON** The tour has come around so quickly. One minute it was, 'Oh, we have a tour at the end of January.' The next minute it was 10 days before the tour starts. (Yes, 10 days!) The rehearsals are going well. The first two days were just constant singing and dancing, from 9am to 8pm, and we learnt five or six routines. Two days later, we've learnt the whole tour. It's not polished and there's loads more to do, but we're making good time. It's been really frantic and busy, but we're loving it. Everybody is learning really quickly. Our choreographer is one of our original dancers from *The X Factor*. We liked his style and decided to go for him. He'll be dancing with us on the tour as well.

sunday 24 january

• JB It's two days before the tour starts and I'm really excited! I was a bit annoyed at the start of rehearsals, because I would have liked to have had more time to prepare. I didn't like the thought of tightening up the show while we were on the road; it's poor form. When people come to a show, they rightly expect it to be a finished and complete show. So I felt that it was important to perfect the choreography before the first date. Fortunately, everything has come together really well. I'm surprised at how much we've picked up in such a short time.

wednesday 26 january
Rhyl Empire Theatre

• JB The first show of the tour! It was fantastic. We were prepared; everything was tight and it looked good. Credit to the
boys and the dancers – we did it! And we were well received.
The supporters and fans were absolutely incredible. They
showed a lot of love and made a lot of noise!

• ASTON We've never played to a crowd that was there just for
JLS before. Totally JLS fans. Every single person was here for us
tonight. It's so crazy. The energy of the fans is incredible. The
screams are mad. Everybody was so excited and having a good
time, which is great.

• ORITSÉ The fans spur me on when I'm on stage. Seeing so
many happy girls with their faces lit up, enjoying our music,
makes me feel so amazing. The louder the screams, the more
I get excited; I want to dance harder and I want to sing better.

At T4 Stars 2009, Earls Court, London

It's weird to see our names in lights: 'JLS'. It seems incredible
that a year ago we were supporting Lemar in a lot of these
venues and now we're on our own headline tour. This is
our show and we have two support acts! It's such a major
achievement, something I've always wanted to do since I was
a kid. I used to stand in front of my grandma's mirror in the
bathroom when I was 11 years old, singing tunes to thousands
of imaginary fans, who were all singing along with me. Now I
get to do it for real with my three bandmates. It is a childhood
dream come true.

• JB My favourite part of the show is probably the slower
section, the second section when we do 'If I Ever', 'Crazy For
You', 'Close To You' and 'Only Making Love'. It's a really chilled-
out section of the show and quite emotive as well. I like it when
you can get a bit more personal, a bit less commercial and more

hands-on. And it's partly my favourite because I'm wearing a waistcoat and a bow tie. I love wearing my suits.

Only one thing went wrong tonight, a wardrobe malfunction: there wasn't any velcro on my waistcoat. So it was in my face while I was performing, doing my turns and jumps! Finally I chucked in on the floor and left it there.

• **ASTON** Tonight our manager Phil said, 'Oh, by the way, did you know that your book went to number one in the book charts?' We all started screaming and jumping up and down. 'Why didn't you tell us at the time?' we said.

tuesday 2 february
'Everybody Hurts' is released in aid
of the victims of the Haiti earthquake

• **ORITSÉ** News of the earthquake in Haiti really affected us. It was terrible to think of all those people dying and getting hurt. Then my cousins in Canada called and said, 'Oritsé, did you know that you've got cousins in Haiti? We've been trying to get hold of them, but we're starting to fear the worst.'

I was shocked. The tragedy had suddenly become much more personal to me. 'We have to do something to help,' I told the guys. 'Somehow we must be able to use our position to raise money.'

That same day we heard through our management that Simon Cowell was organising the Help Haiti single. We immediately got in touch with Simon: 'Please let us contribute to the record! It's a really, really important cause for us.'

• **MARVIN** To hear that Oritsé had family in Haiti was heart-breaking. We had given a donation – as you would when a country needs help, and as people did all over the world – but when we heard about Oritsé's family, we wanted to do something to make a real difference. Performing on the single was the best way we could contribute and we recorded the vocals at the end of January. We were pleased we could help, but it was a sad day.

• JB It's hard to picture what it's like to lose your house, your home, or your family. Imagine if you lost everything that was familiar to you, everything that you understood. It's a terrible thought, which is why we wanted to give a helping hand. We couldn't physically go out there and help, but we offered what we could. Individually, I made a donation and as a group we could offer our expertise. Everybody on the single was showing their love to the people who had experienced this tragedy.

saturday 6 february
Manchester Apollo

At the 'One Shot' video shoot

• **ORITSÉ** I nearly fainted tonight while I was singing 'Beat It' by Michael Jackson. Everything felt normal while I was dancing and then suddenly the room started swirling around in slow motion. As I fell backwards, a voice inside me was already saying, 'Oritsé, get up!' I hit the floor, but then launched myself back up and went on with my routine. I don't think the crowd noticed. I was shaking a bit, but I managed to hide it.

It was a combination of exhaustion, not eating enough and lack of water, I think. Rest is more important than I realised; I mustn't keep staying up late and playing guitar. I had to sort myself out very quickly and I am now eating regularly, drinking lots of water and getting plenty of sleep!

sunday 7 february
Sheffield City Hall and Memorial Hall

• **MARVIN** A rubbish day for me, because I ran on stage the wrong way. I was meant to go round the back and then upstairs and down some other stairs, but because it was so dark, I couldn't see and I went in the wrong direction. Then I slipped over and hit my head on the floor, which really hurt. But I quickly jumped up, ran all the way around the back and arrived on stage late. It was a big palaver and must have looked pretty comic to any onlookers. Our security guy was really laughing at me.

sunday 14 february
Valentine's Day, Liverpool Empire

• **ASTON** Yesterday was definitely a birthday to remember, the best birthday I've ever had! I was 22 years old! But it was a very long day, because we had a matinee show at the Hammersmith Apollo for Nokia competition winners followed by an evening show.

• **JB** The Nokia gig was an unusual gig, with more of a corporate vibe than we're used to. It wasn't our most vocal audience! They might have liked us, but they are not the types to stand up and scream. It was more restrained, with people sitting down, taking it in and observing, very different to playing to a crowd of girls with their hands outstretched! It was good, though.

• **MARVIN** The evening show was amazing, as all of our family were there. I looked out into the crowd and saw that my mum had tears in her eyes as she watched us. It was really an emotional day for her. Plus, it was Aston's birthday!

• JB Mostly I haven't been that nervous on this tour, but I was nervous last night, because there were a lot of people we knew out in the crowd. Plus, half the choreographic world was there! Some of Cheryl's dancers had tickets: we are talking the hottest dancers in the industry. We knew they would be making judgements on our performance, on the show and our choreography, and of course we wanted to live up to their expectations.

There's a suprise, JB on his phone

It's one thing hearing the opinions of people who don't know the ins and outs of performing, but when you are performing to people who do understand it, you feel you need to achieve another level of respect and showmanship. It was a bit daunting, especially as we'd had a long day and it was a bit hectic. But our label manager and management said that it was definitely the best show so far.

We've had a lot of people coming in to review the show. The *Independent* gave us four stars; it was incredible to get such a good write-up from a broadsheet, as opposed to a tabloid. I was pleased, because I want our music to reach everybody. People tell us that our target audience is 14-year-olds, but actually it's everyone. Our older fans may not be so vocal. They may not write the reviews on YouTube or on the website but they are still our supporters; they still buy their children our records and listen to our music on the radio. We don't want to exclude any part of the market.

> • Aston Last night's show set the tone for the whole tour. It was mad. The energy that came from the crowd was indescribable. It spurred us on to perform bigger than ever. It was nice for everyone's families to be there and we just gave it that little bit extra. But I actually got quite embarrassed when the crowd sang me 'Happy Birthday'. I don't usually get embarrassed, but I had to stand there while they sang it and I was thinking, Oh dear!

• **MARVIN** After the show, the boys and I went to a club to celebrate. We had a very good night which went on into this morning. Then we slept a few hours, woke up and came to Liverpool.

• **ASTON** All my friends from London and Peterborough were already in the club by the time we arrived. The Saturdays and Sugababes were there, some of the sexiest girls in pop music at the moment! We were supposed to go to Frankie's birthday, but we were working and couldn't make it, so it was great that she made it to mine. Chipmunk was meant to come down, but he was working on his tour.

• JB The club was a bit too packed, but it was a great night and Aston enjoyed himself. We were well looked after and the company was fantastic.

monday 15 february

• **MARVIN** Every show is special, but it was extra special doing a show on Valentine's Day last night. I sent a Valentine's card to one girl … perhaps you can guess who. It was nothing special, just a nice card. She sent me one too, of course!

• **ASTON** It was a lonely Valentine's Day for me. It was a bit weird. I'm not saying that I didn't get any text messages or offers to go out, but I couldn't go anywhere because of the tour. Not that I minded, because I'd had my birthday and seen everybody I cared about.

I didn't send any Valentine's texts or cards. There was no romance, except with the Liverpool crowd, the prettiest crowd of girls on the whole tour, ironically. Every single girl in the audience was stunning. Hopefully, I made someone in the front happy by giving her a rose.

Someone asked me the other day if I ever get bored with fans screaming and shouting at me. Bored? No way. I will never, ever be sick of girls' attention!

• JB I didn't send any Valentines and I feel bad that I didn't. I usually get a card for my mum, but even she didn't get a card, and how can I send anybody else a card, if she didn't get one? I should have sent one or two, but if I'm going to be 100 per cent honest, I didn't have any time to go shopping.

I like picking out my own card and presents; I don't like people to do it for me. But something always seemed to get in the way – we didn't get back from Manchester until the early hours on Friday, then we had rehearsals from 10am until 8pm. Saturday should have been a good day for shopping, but we had to get our hair cut at the Hammersmith Apollo in between shows. Then yesterday we were in Liverpool. And yesterday was Valentine's Day! So my Valentine's card was a cyber card this year, I'm afraid. I had to send an eValentine to my girlfriend instead.

tuesday 16 february
The Brits, Earls Court, London

• ORITSÉ What an incredible night! We've won two Brits and we are elated! There's lots of punching the air going on. Plus, I met Mel B, which made me go weak at the knees, and Geri Halliwell, who is also totally gorgeous.

• ASTON This morning I opened the dressing-room door and Lily Allen walked in, wearing a T-shirt with a photo of her breasts on it. Then the boobs moved! The photo was in fact a piece of see-through material! Nice, very nice. I didn't say anything, but I couldn't help but stare. I was trying not to, but it happened. She must have known what she was doing, so she was just playing with us. I'm definitely an admirer of hers.

We also saw the Spice Girls. We all took a bit of a fancy to Mel B when she came past. She was looking very nice indeed. It was funny seeing her and Oritsé. She pointed at him and said something like, 'You are really sexy.' I think it made his year!

In a singing voice...

♪ Jason Deruloooo! ♪

• **MARVIN** Another highlight was when Robbie Williams went out of his way to come up to me and Aston. 'Congratulations!' he said, 'I was gutted when you guys beat us to number one for the album, but you really deserved it.'

Next we bumped into Cheryl, bless her. She was really happy for us and there was some friendly banter about going up against us for Best Single. She is a sweetheart, a lovely girl. We are always going to have her full support.

Then, as we were walking to the stage, Jay-Z walked straight through the middle of us! 'Yeah, Jay-Z!' we said. We love his music.

It was actually really chilled backstage during the day. We had massages, manicures and hair washes. We pampered ourselves for a couple of hours. We weren't nervous about the performance, because we are so used to performing. But it made us nervous to have so many important people around us, from our management and record company to the head of Sony, who came in to see us. There was also a record company boss from the US who had specifically come along to see us perform, so that added to the pressure. We didn't get to meet him, but the feedback was fantastic.

• **ASTON** I loved our Armani get-ups. My first tailored Armani suit! We had to go for fittings and we got to keep them, along with the stage outfits. We got to keep everything.

• **ORITSÉ** I love our suits, but I can't help remembering how I used to buy all my clothes from charity shops before we went on *The X Factor*. Yet everyone thought I dressed really well back then. It just shows that you don't have to go to the best designers to look good.

• **ASTON** We had a day and a half of rehearsals, but I was so nervous it was unbelievable. It was unusual for me. All day we were being told about the important people who would be watching us. I actually texted my mum and dad and said, 'I'm really nervous.'

My dad texted back, 'Don't be stupid. Do what you were born to do.'

My nerves turned into good nerves half an hour before the performance, thankfully.

At T4 Stars 2009, Earls Court, London

• **JB** It was a bit of a weird day. We turned up, did a couple of interviews, did a rehearsal and after that there was a long lull. Someone brought us some gifts, including watches and Mulberry holdalls, which was incredible; then I tried to get an hour's sleep, because I'm still tired from Aston's birthday and have a cold. I really wasn't feeling well, but I started to feel better as the day went on. At about half-past four we had something to eat and did some press with the guys from Capital and Radio 1. Then we got changed into our suits and went outside in order to come back inside and do the whole red carpet thing. It was weird to be doing something I've seen people like Rihanna and Justin Timberlake do.

It was raining, which was a bit of a shame. We would have liked to have stayed there and signed autographs for all the people who came out to see us. They'd been waiting there for hours and some of them were soaked to the bone, when they could have been at home in the warm, watching the Brits on TV. They sacrifice so much for us! We always want to give as much time and as much of ourselves as we can to the people who come to support us.

• **ORITSÉ** Tonight I experienced a sense of déjà vu as fans chased our car down the street. That was me once, I thought. A few years ago, at the same venue, I went to the World Music Awards and saw Michael Jackson perform. I remember waiting outside, watching the stars go down the red carpet, saying to myself, 'One day I'm going to be there, in my own right, as an artist.'

When Michael Jackson made a getaway down the Earls Court Road afterwards, I was one of the fans running after his car, knocking on his window and yelling. I saw a gap in the car window and shouted through it, 'Oritsé, Oritsé, Oritsé!' just to let him know I existed. I wanted him to notice me. I wanted him to remember my name and face in years to come, if I became a performing artist.

With choreographer Jeri Slaughter

The Great "Jeri Slaughter"

As a fan, you always hope that you will get noticed. That's why I spend so much time with my fans – because I know what it feels like. I sign autographs, take pictures, have conversations and read their emails, messages and letters. I can't read everything or see everyone, but I make sure I take home any letter that I do intercept. Once I spent three days going through a huge pile of letters, replying to as many as I could. I love the fans unconditionally. Without them, I would be nothing.

I would have loved Michael Jackson to see how we are contributing to pop music and trying to keep his genre of music going. To meet him would have been an absolute dream come true, but now that will never happen. As time passes, I appreciate him and his artistry more and more. I'm studying him on my computer and on YouTube all the time now. There are two rooms on either side of the tour bus and I often lock myself in one of them to go through his videos and listen to his music. I know so much of it by heart, but even when you've seen something of his a hundred times, there is always something you haven't noticed. That's how brilliant he was. I didn't think about winning an award tonight. I was totally focused on giving the best possible, groundbreaking, epic performance that I could give, alongside my band members. My love is for the stage and for entertaining. That is what I'm most passionate about. If we hadn't won any awards at all, I still would have walked away happy and proud, because we gave the performance of our lives.

We started the performance suspended in the air. I'll never forget the feeling in my heart as the drums started up. I felt pretty emotional as I looked left and right at the others. I was thinking: Look what we are doing! Look how far we have come! From a cramped little rehearsal room that we struggled to rent for a day to literally hanging above a world stage in front of thousands of people and internationally respected artists. What an incredible journey we are on.

As I started singing, I wanted to become the music, *be* the music. Zone in! I told myself, this is for you, Mummy. It was pretty special; I knew my mum was watching and I wanted to give my performance something extra, just for her.

*oritsé at it again...
who got his heart
this time ?!*

• JB We felt we had more chance in the Best Breakthrough Act category, because there were only around five nominees. But then you've got to consider the other nominees: Pixie Lott has had a fantastic year and gone from strength to strength; all her singles have gone to number one. She is a great talent and a great vocalist. Then there's Florence and the Machine, who have also had a great year. There were so many great people in the category that you couldn't tell who was going to win. The funny thing is that we know all these guys really well. They also have great support from the radio stations, which helps them with their promotion.

When it came to Best British Single, we couldn't take anything for granted, because there have been some huge singles this year. There was Alexandra's fantastic song, 'Bad Boys', and 'Fight For This Love' by Cheryl Cole was the biggest single of the year. If you go on statistics and sales, Cheryl should have won the award, because she outsold us. Tinchy Stryder and N-Dubz also had a fantastic single with 'Number one' so to assume we would win would have been foolish. 'Beat Again' was only at the top for two weeks. All these things go on in your mind; you just don't know what is going to happen.

• **MARVIN** I don't think I can put into words how amazing and crazy tonight was. It was the biggest and most successful night of our lives. We didn't have a clue what the results were going to be. Before the first award was announced for Best Breakthrough Act, I sat at the table with my fists clenched, willing it to happen. When our name was called out by Geri Halliwell, the feeling was just incredible. Can it get any better? I thought. It feels like all the hard work, persistence and attention to detail has paid off.

• **ASTON** When Geri Halliwell gave us an award, I managed to say something, say thank you to some people. I can't even remember getting the second one, just that I ran down the plank and did a back flip. I left JB to do the talking.

• **MARVIN** We thanked Simon Cowell on stage because he has been a big supporter of JLS from day one. If it wasn't for him giving us the opportunity to go through all of the rounds on *The X Factor*, we wouldn't be here. He gave birth to JLS. We will always be in debt to *The X Factor* and we'll never forget it.

• **JB** Winning Best Single was especially good because we really respect Steve Mac and Wayne Hector, who wrote 'Beat Again'. I think it was their first Brit Award, which is amazing when you think that these guys have been working for 20-odd years with different acts across the county and the world. We've known Wayne for a while, since before we did *The X Factor*, because he worked with Marvin when he was in VS. Later, Steve Mac really got behind us. I remember him saying that he wanted us to be the best and if he could help us do that, he'd be happy. Well, we're all happy now! My mum and dad and brother were there to see us perform. My mum messaged me afterwards: 'Absolutely fantastic!' She wanted us to win everything, of course, but didn't think it was our time to win Best Group yet. Still, she was convinced that we would win at least two awards. When she was proved right, she was over the moon for us. She came to the party to celebrate with us and met our label and management.

• **ASTON** My parents left me messages screaming down the phone, but it still hasn't hit home yet that we won two awards. When they are delivered and we put them up in our house and look at them, then it will hit us. For now, it is a big blur.

wednesday 17 february

• **ASTON** We went to the label party afterwards and congratulated all the people behind the scenes. What a great year! Then it was on to the Jay-Z after party and we had a little drink with Jay-Z. Before we left, I stole Jay-Z's dressing-room marker. I'm going to frame it and put it on my wall. I'm still a fan!

• **JB** I wasn't really in the mood when I got to the club after the Sony party, because we had been drinking since about 10pm. Then Jay-Z sent us over four bottles of his own brand champagne, a bottle each, and my cousin Mark, my friend Miles and I finished the whole bottle between us. Everyone was cool, though; nobody was stumbling about or falling out of the club and I didn't get to bed until 5am!

thursday 18 february
Bristol Colston Hall

• **ORITSÉ** I was in shock when I saw the headline in the *Sun* today: 'Jay-Z bigz up JLS'. After seeing us perform, he told a reporter, 'They put on a class performance and I think they will go on to be as big as 'N Sync.'

How fabulous! I look up to Jay-Z in so many ways, especially for being a musical entrepreneur. I'm very driven and ambitious in the same way he is and I'd love to emulate his success. I've watched all the documentaries about him and I've seen how hard he works. For someone like him to really give us the thumbs up is pretty surreal.

• JB I'm really tired! I didn't get a chance to sleep on the bus yesterday because I was calling and texting everybody, thanking them for supporting us. I was feeling a bit under the weather as well. Yesterday's show wasn't my best. But I had 12 hours' sleep last night. Lovely! Whenever the tiredness builds up, I like to have a night in and not see anyone and chill out and relax. Marvin and Aston's brothers are with us for the next couple of days, but I know them well enough to say hi and bye, and go to bed.

friday 19 february

• MARVIN Last night I went on my first official date with Rochelle, to the Ivy restaurant. We hit it off, as usual. We really get on! I let her know how I felt about her. I think – I hope – she feels the same. She has agreed to go on another date . . .

monday 22 february
Manchester Apollo

• JB We haven't had any days off for ages. We did the Haiti single on one of our days off, the album chart show on another, the Brit rehearsals on another. Plus, we've been working hard to promote our new single, 'One Shot', which comes out today. It is a case of working non-stop until we finish the tour on 8 March. I need to go away then. I'm looking for somewhere that is reasonably hot and not too far, not more than five hours on a plane.

I'm still exhilarated about the Brits but, as the boys will tell you, nothing ever really sinks in, whether it's the number one single, the number one album or the day we heard that we'd sold a million records. I don't really want all these achievements to sink in either, because it would be quite easy to think, Hey, we won two Brits, so the show tonight doesn't matter.

Tonight's show really matters! We'll be up in front of the fans and supporters who voted for us to win the Brits. They've paid money to come and watch the show and we are going to give them their money's worth.

• **ORITSÉ** Tonight while I was dancing to 'Beat Again', I looked down at my feet and both my trainers had come off. I was dancing on stage in my socks! 'Keep going, Oritsé, just keep dancing,' I told myself. I couldn't start fiddling about with my shoes, so I went on with the routine and soon forgot about my trainers.

tuesday 23 february
Blackpool Opera House

• **ORITSÉ** Tonight I met a woman and her young daughter after the show. The mum was in tears as she told me how her daughter had been attacked. I felt so, so upset for them. What a crushing, devastating thing to happen.

Then she said that her daughter had found herself again through our music. 'You won't understand, but you have literally given me back my daughter,' she sobbed.

I nearly broke down. I didn't realise how much of an influence we have on people. I had to keep myself together and be strong for her, so I hugged her and said, 'You are so special, do you realise that?' It made me feel a huge responsibility to keep on doing the best I can, because we really do affect people's lives.

tuesday 1 march
Belfast

• JB Last night we had a crew party for everyone on the tour upstairs at Cafe Vaudeville in Belfast. It was the end-of-tour party: even though it's not quite the end of the tour, it's the only chance there was for everyone to get together. It was quite empty because it was a Monday night, but it was cool. We were able to say thank you to all the people we don't often see, because they're usually putting things up or taking them down after we've danced and jumped all over them. It's not a big crew, so we chatted to everyone.

O.M.GGGG!!!

Tomorrow morning we're taking a private jet from Ireland to Kent. We're being flown in to shoot an advert for Walkers Crisps. It will be my first trip in a private jet, but definitely not the last, I hope!

I used to want to be a pilot. My mum and dad bought me flying lessons for my fifteenth birthday and I was co-pilot in a Cessna a couple of times. One day, the pilot handed the control of the plane over to me and I did a loop the loop! It felt a bit weird, but I loved it. One day I will definitely do it again.

tuesday 2 march
Sandwich, Kent

• MARVIN We were really excited when we found out that Walkers had approached us to appear in one of their TV commercials. Walkers make very distinctive adverts with huge stars, so it was a real honour. We instantly agreed!

We took a private jet from Belfast to Sandwich in Kent this morning at 5am. Sounds glamorous, doesn't it? But in fact the plane was tiny! It was so small that we couldn't fit all of our luggage inside. It was just us and two security guys: one of them is 6ft 6in – I don't know how he managed to cram his body into the plane!

We had been told that we would be filmed from the moment we arrived, so there was a camera crew waiting when we touched down on the private landing strip and we were filmed getting off the plane. We felt like movie stars! It was a freezing cold day, though – which slightly took the edge off!

Also appearing in the ad are Frank Lampard, the Chelsea football player, Jenson Button, the Formula 1 racing driver, Marco Pierre White, the chef, and Pamela Anderson, *Baywatch* star! The idea is that we all live in one town – Pamela Anderson is the local barmaid and Jenson Button drives a taxi, etc. We met Jenson Button today because we filmed a couple of scenes with him, but none of the others were there.

Our role is to surprise a group of school kids by turning up at their school and performing. We actually did surprise them, too. They had been told that someone was coming in to talk to them about government funding or something boring like that – and then we were introduced instead. They all went crazy! It was really fun.

• JB I've just heard that 'One Shot' has sold 200,000 copies! And our album has gone quadruple platinum and sold more than a million copies! I'm speechless.

monday 8 march

• **Marvin** The tour is over! It wasn't too long. It wasn't too short. It felt just right, the icing on the cake of all our achievements, a way to give back to all the fans. I'm actually pleased, in all honesty, because we've been on the road for six weeks. It's been amazing and we've had an incredible response from every city we've visited, but now it's time for a break.

It feels like the end of chapter one for JLS, a defining moment. The first album is out, the singles have been released and the tour promoting the first album is over. Now we're going on holiday and when we get back, we'll be starting work on our second album.

> • JB The end of the tour marks the end of an era and the end of the first campaign as a group: the album, the three singles, the radio tours, the tour, the MOBOs, the Brits. I've always liked performing, but I'm really looking forward to getting back in the studio and writing.

> > • **Marvin** We can't wait for the arena tour later in the year. Performing is the best part of being in JLS and being on tour is like being in a bubble. You live in hotels, so there are no worries about what's going on back at home. Plus, you are with your mates and your family come and see you all the time. The next tour will be another first: our first arena tour. Again, we will have to think long and hard about the type of show we put on and how to make it better than ever.

• **Oritsé** I'm sad that the tour has ended. Touring is addictive; you don't want it to stop, even when you're tired. I really appreciated the final days and I wanted to give it my absolute best, partly because it was our first-ever tour and we'll never be able to say that again. I know I'm going to miss the high of performing and the energy we get from the fans. That is definitely the best bit.

thursday 11 march

• **ASTON** For me, the tour didn't actually feel like it had ended until I was on holiday in Dubai with my two friends, sitting by the pool in this hotel. Until then, I kept waiting for someone to say, 'It's time for the sound check,' or, 'You're going for an interview now.'

This has been a relaxing holiday with no partying at all. I'm not living up to my party name! I'm in bed before 12 every night and I'm getting 12 hours' sleep every day. The only exciting thing I've done is to shave my hair off! It was my holiday dare. I've been threatening to do it for a year now, because whenever we're getting ready for a TV appearance and we have our hair cut, Oritsé puts his hat on and JB and Marvin are done, because they have short hair.

'Let's go,' they say.

'Wait, I need to do my hair,' I say.

'OK, do your hair . . .' they sigh.

'You know what?' I say. 'I'm going to shave my head and then you'll be sorry!'

I think they're going to say, 'Oh dear!' when they see what I've done, but it'll be all right. It grows quickly.

• **MARVIN** I'm having an amazing holiday in Dubai, just doing nothing! It was a long tour, so it's important to recharge the batteries. I was expecting my voice to be tired more than anything else, but it turns out that it's my body that's exhausted after all that dancing. It's been good to be able to sit in the sun and chill for a few days. Now I'm itching to get back to work, though! I can't wait to see the boys and crack on with chapter two.

• **ORITSÉ** Finally, I've had some time to spend with my family! I've really missed them. My mum is happy, but her illness goes up and down, which is hard. My brothers are with her most of the time. They are a great support to her and my little sister, so I feel she is looked after. I used to worry about her because you always feel that nobody can look after your mum better than you can, but they are doing a great job.

s u n d a y   1 4   m a r c h

• **ORITSÉ** I'm at a spa in the countryside, winding down for a few days. Lots of swimming, relaxation and massages – yes! Having hot stone therapy was nice and I really enjoyed the seaweed bath when they wrap you up in clingfilm, but my favourite treatment was called holistic therapy. I thought I was going for a regular massage, but suddenly the massage therapist started massaging my head and saying, 'You are in your own space. Enjoy the moment now. You are the root of a tree . . .' and all this kind of stuff.

I thought it was funny at first, but then I really got into it. I even went back for another treatment the next day. I think the therapist was proud of herself, because she calmed my energy and spirit. The boys always say that I'm bit of a workaholic and it's true, I suppose. I never really want to take a break or go on holiday, because I'm caught up in the momentum of doing something I really love. I get so excited and I don't want it to stop. I'm always saying, 'Come on, what can we do next? Let's do something else. I know, let's bungee jump for charity!'

Yesterday all these women came up to me and said, 'You're from JLS, aren't you? You're from JLS!'

'Me? JLS?' I said. 'No, I'm Usher.'

They looked at me for a moment. 'Usher? Oh, yes, that makes much more sense. Of course, you're Usher!'

I thought, Are you being serious? It was pretty funny.

● JB I'm in Morocco on holiday with my family, staying in a riad for a week. It's perfect, fantastic. I wanted to go somewhere I've never been before, somewhere warm, but not too far away. It's not exactly hot, but it's a lot warmer than it is in England. And the food is incredible! The lunches in the riad are so good that one couple staying here have been taking notes from the chef.

In the *X Factor* dressing room

It's Mother's Day today and I didn't wake up until 5pm! Luckily, Mum understands that I'm catching up on my sleep after a long tour – and we're going out to dinner tonight. I gave her some flowers before we came away, too.

I haven't done much sightseeing while I've been here. I had a little walk around Marrakech one afternoon and I went quad biking yesterday, but you know what I'm like with my sleep! At the moment, I'm going to take any chance I have to sleep. So I'll have to save the sightseeing for next time.

tuesday 16 march

● **ORITSÉ** Our personal assistant, Erica, asked me to come to a meeting today. She arrived all suited up and there was champagne on the table. I was alarmed to see that there were tears in her eyes. 'Erica, why are you crying?' I asked.

'The Multiple Sclerosis Society want to award you with the MS Inspiration Award, for all the work you have done to raise awareness about MS,' she said, hardly able to get the words out.

Hearing this, I became quite emotional. I couldn't believe it, because it's the biggest, highest honour ever. Apparently the award is given out by the Prime Minister and his wife, but I had no idea it even existed. Raising awareness of MS is just something I'm passionate about because my mum's got MS.

The award is a secret for now. The only reason I've been told about it is because it will be presented at a ceremony on 22 April, when I'll be in America. So I'll go to the MS society headquarters in North London to accept the award on camera instead.

wednesday 17 march

• **MARVIN** Aston and I have spent the last two days cleaning up our house, which isn't very pop star-ish! It's really brought us down to earth. I had my Marigolds on! We've been living here for about 15 months now and it got to the point when the flat was literally upside down with junk. We never seem to have time to properly clean and de-clutter the place and it was incredibly messy. I'm a bit of a clean freak and it was getting a bit too much for me, so it's been very liberating. I bagged up about eight black bags and Aston had about six black bags, mainly clothes, which we've given to our friends and family.

• **ASTON** That was hard work! It was a long way from my ideal weekend, which would start with a relaxing, non-drinking party on a Friday night. I'd get up at midday to early afternoon on the Saturday and meet the boys at a venue like the O2, where we'd put on the best show ever, in the best atmosphere, and afterwards go out with friends to celebrate and party hard. On the Sunday, I'd have a relaxing day, maybe go shopping, go out for dinner with friends and chill on Sunday night, getting ready for work on Monday.

• **JB** Mine would be to have Friday off and sleep in late, go shopping, to Nando's and the cinema. Saturday: I'd sleep in late, go to lunch in the afternoon, go to dinner and maybe go out to a club, if I was in the mood (I'm not usually in the mood). Then on Sunday I'd go to church in the morning if I wasn't too tired and eat Sunday lunch with the family, then have a couple of glasses of wine and watch a film in the evening.

• **ORITSÉ** I'd start my ideal weekend sitting at home on the couch, drinking hot chocolate, watching movies and snuggling up to a nice young lady. I'd spend the Sunday with my family, all of us laughing, playing loud music, singing, dancing, joking around, eating good food and having lots of fun.

• **MARVIN** I'd do a little bit of shopping, go to the cinema, go to the theatre, go out for a nice meal and some drinks in a bar, and on Sunday spend time with my family and my baby nephew, Harvey.

thursday 18 march

• **MARVIN** It's my birthday and I'm 25!

Exactly a year ago, our label manager, Nick Raphael, called me up and said, 'Happy Birthday, Marvin. I've got a birthday present for you.' I thought he meant a wallet or something, but he said, 'Check your email.'

His email was entitled, 'Forever And A Day' and attached was the track that later became 'Everybody In Love'. The moment I heard it, I just knew it was going to be a number one. What a great birthday present!

Today Nick texted me again. 'I have another birthday present for you,' he said. This time it was a song called, 'The Club Is Alive'. I've just listened to it and it's given me the same goose bump feeling that I had with 'Everybody In Love'. It is definitely a hit.

Tonight I'm going to my favourite restaurant, Gilgamesh, in Camden. The most important people in my life are coming: my mum, my dad, my brother, Aston, JB, Oritsé and my good friend Tom and his girlfriend.

• **ASTON** I keep telling Marvin that he is a quarter of a century old, as it sounds older than 25! It's really annoying him. Ah, but he gives it back to me as much as I give it to him. It's not a one-way thing.

friday 19 march
Sport Relief, BBC studios, London

• **MARVIN** Tonight we sang Lemar's song, 'What About Love' with Lemar; it was the first time we've sung a ballad on TV since *The X Factor*. Lemar is a legend in our eyes; we're in awe of how good he is and how long he has been in the industry. He helped us out by taking us on tour with him just after *The X Factor*, so it felt right to do a song together.

• **ASTON** Here's a funny story: when I was 14, my friend and I went to a Justin Timberlake concert, not knowing that Lemar was supporting him. I was a massive Lemar fan at the time and 'What About Love' was my all-time favourite Lemar song. When we got to the concert, we were hanging around in the foyer when we suddenly heard Lemar's first single, 'Dance With You', coming from the auditorium. We looked at each other and said, 'No way!' and ran in to watch our idol. So I've gone from watching Lemar support Justin Timberlake to supporting him on his tour and then singing with him. It's a very long way; it's crazy!

• **MARVIN** The performance went really well and then we went out and celebrated my birthday at a nightclub called Alto. Rochelle came, as did Pixie Lott and Amelle and Jade from the Sugababes. Aston's dad and my dad were there, too. They had their own table and there were bottles of champagne and rum everywhere. I wouldn't usually go to a nightclub with my dad, but you know what? I was like, 'Get the old man out!'

• ASTON I was trying to chat a girl up and my dad got in my way! He had drunk quite a bit more than we had and he kept putting his arm around me and saying things like, 'Your mum and I are so proud of you . . .'

'Look, Dad, it's not the time to talk about this now!' I said.

Someone was walking around with a snake in the club. 'Get that away from me!' I said, because I hate snakes.

• JB I wasn't cool with the snake. I don't actually mind snakes and I like watching them on TV, but I don't like it when people put them round your neck. At least it was a boa constrictor, which isn't as scary as a venomous snake. Venomous snakes tend to move very fast, which is what I don't like about them! But apart from the snake, it was a wicked night. Everybody had a great time.

• MARVIN I tried to invite as many people as I could: all of my friends from work and my old friends from school and people who I haven't seen for a long time, who are always having a go at me because I don't have time to see them. We had our own private room, which was brilliant. It was really nice to catch up with people.

Best of all, though, Rochelle and I have gone on loads of dates now and I would say that I'm extremely happy and she is extremely happy as well. She is a great girl and a dream girlfriend. She is beautiful and she has her head screwed on. She has a great family. She is in the industry, so she understands how it works; we understand each other very well. So we will see how it goes. I'm a lucky boy.

• **ORITSÉ** I am also dating someone at the moment: she is a performer who used to be a dancer. We have a lot of fun and it's nice dating, but I don't feel I can get serious at this point in time. I'm not tied down or committed. The only things I'm committed to are my music and my fans. My fans are my true love.

• **ASTON** I'm dating as much as I can, but when it comes to going out with girls, I don't always want to go out and be photographed, so sometimes I'll just ask a girl to come round for dinner at the house. I do the same with my friends who are girls. I've got loads of girl mates who say, 'Let's go out for dinner like we used to.' The problem is that a lot of them are stunning to look at, so the moment I'm seen out with them, everyone assumes I'm having a relationship with them.

• JB I've been with my girlfriend for a while now. She is lovely, very special. She lives in Epsom, about 15 minutes from me, and I see her all the time. We often go out to dinner, or to the cinema, or to Nando's, or we chill out at mine or hers. I like the way she thinks. To me that is more important than what you wear or how much money you earn. It's about how you approach life and I think she has her priorities right. Does she make me laugh? Well, she thinks she does!

• **ASTON** I haven't partied hard for a long time now. I haven't really been in the mood. It is getting a lot harder to go out and have a normal night without random people coming up and asking, 'Can I have a picture?' or sidling up to your table to have a drink. Of course, it's nice that people want a photo, but sometimes I just want to focus on having a good time with my friends.

I've been having the boys over and it's been just like the old days, with people falling asleep in the living room downstairs. We've been staying up until 4am talking about old times and ex girlfriends over a couple of beers. It's just boy talk – and JLS talk. 'Have you met this girl? Have you met that girl?' 'Yeah!'

My friends are all at university now and every bit as busy as I am, studying and sitting exams. Some of them have six-hour exams! That's my idea of torture. I used to hate just sitting at a desk, writing. But my friends are good at it and they love it. They're happy studying for hours on end in the library and writing essays, whereas I just couldn't do it. It's funny how different people doing different things can get on so well.

It's nice when we're all together, the lads having a chat. I can mess around and have a joke, without thinking, Oh, I shouldn't have said that because the camera is on me. I can just be myself and totally relax.

Triceps Neeeeow"

• **ORITSÉ** When I'm on my own, I often pluck away at my guitar, trying to practise, or I watch movies. But mainly I plan how I'm going to take over the world. When I'm with my friends, I like to go out to live music nights. I love going to the cinema too, but I have to disguise myself when I go!

sunday 28 march

• JB We're going to LA tomorrow! We are going to be working with some new people in the studio, some great people, so I can't wait. I was talking to Oritsé the other day about what I love about the studio. Number one is the creative side of it; number two, I feel I am good at it; and number three is that I'm into the idea of ownership. It's intellectual property, isn't it? Any song we write is an asset. We own it; it belongs to us.

People often ask how I prepare before going into the studio. Well, it depends. There are a few ways to do it. You can go into the studio with a top-line writer, a songwriter who already has a concept for a song and will already have written a couple of choruses of a song. If we like the way it's going, we'll expand on the idea, write the verses and finish the song off.

When you start with a fresh song, which Oritsé and Marvin are doing today, you have to be prepared and go in with the concept that you either feel passionately about or feel is missing from the album. It might be an up-tempo song, a ballad or something mid-tempo. There are so many different options. Ballads are easier to write, because they are emotive and most people have had an emotive experience, even if it's a negative one. You might not have even experienced love, for instance, but you could still write about not finding love.

When it comes to writing an up-tempo song, you can't always make it a love song. So what do you write about? Do you write about something close to you, something personal to you? And if you don't draw on something personal, what knowledge or experience do you draw on to make the song good enough? I'm learning all the time.

• **ORITSÉ** I can't wait to go to America. I've dreamed of having a music career around the world ever since I was a little boy. Plus, the artists that I'm influenced by or who I look up to are predominantly American. One day I'd love to live in LA. There is just a different standard out there, and I love the vibe there, and the mentality. People are so driven. Everyone is engrossed by what they are doing.

• **MARVIN** It's a dream come true to be going to America to write and record our album. And we'll be killing two birds with one stone, because we'll also be promoting 'Everybody In Love' over there. Our second single over here is going to be the first single to be released in America, because it has more of an American vibe than 'Beat Again'. It's well suited to the American market.

Like any artists, we've always aspired to international success, but we never thought that the first stop would be America! It has a reputation of being very difficult for Brits to break, so it's a big deal, even though working with American artists is a lot easier than it was. The music industry is a lot smaller these days and the Internet and YouTube mean that our music is accessible to everyone. I think Simon Cowell has a lot to do with it as well. He's as big in America as he is over here.

Rihanna has been quoted as saying that she will perform a duet with us this year, and she has also said that Jay-Z wants to work with us. Apparently she wants to get close to me, but you never know what to believe! We'd love to perform a duet with her. That would be incredible. We are working on it. Obviously, a collaboration with Jay-Z would be great too. All of these things just seem crazy, but hopefully they will happen.

I'm looking forward to getting back to LA. This time around we are recording and writing out there. We are staying in our favourite hotel, The Mondrian, and then we're going to be touring the radio stations for three weeks.

We will effectively be starting from scratch because nobody knows us in the US. That's fine. We are not scared of hard work. It's going to be really good recording the second album and any success we have with 'Everybody In Love' will be a bonus.

• **ASTON** I'm probably looking forward to this trip more than anyone. I'm so excited! I loved LA the last time we were there. The food, the girls, the sun, the people we'll be working with: it's going to be the best trip ever.

I have high hopes for the writing of the second album. We're going to be working with people who have worked with Ne-Yo and Beyoncé, the biggest stars in the world. I'm also looking forward to promoting 'Everybody In Love'. People keep saying that there are no boy bands in America at the moment and so they're ready and waiting for us over there. So we are going for it in a major way. You never know what could happen . . .

thursday 15 april
Los Angeles

• **Marvin** Recording has been going very well. We've had some great writing sessions. Myself and JB, Wayne Hector and Toby Gad (who produced 'If I Was A Boy' for Beyoncé) have written a really, really good song called 'Every Day I Love You A Little Bit More'. We're confident that it's going to be on the album. We've worked with some amazing people and come up with some great results.

• JB The studios are a little bit different here – Toby Gad has a swimming pool in the courtyard of his studio! I was supposed to go swimming there a couple of days ago, but I changed to a different studio at the last minute. Oh well, next time!

• **Aston** We're having a GREAT time! We've written 15 tracks already, and some of them are very strong. For me, it feels like we're working at a different level out here. Everyone's really on it and passionate about what they're doing, which is great for us. There is pressure on us to write a good album, but we're not feeling it so much because we know we're going to get it done.

monday 19 april

• **Oritsé** I tend to put on weight when I'm not in my normal routine, when I'm away from home. That's when I eat too much and don't train enough. So I've been having to work really hard here to keep my weight down and I've been training intensely. I haven't got the best body in the world, but I tell myself I'm getting there.

I definitely feel better when I'm lighter, so when I reach for that late-night doughnut, I ask myself, Is it really worth it, adding 250 calories right now? I remind myself that I'll feel better about myself if I go to sleep and wake up in the morning without having eaten it.

My weight goes up and down all the time, but I try not to feel too bad when it goes up. It's hard at times, because weight is so linked with self-esteem. I'm working in an industry that's very superficial – you're beautiful if you're skinny but if you're bigger, you're not. It's especially in focus for me, because I'm always being looked at and photographed. But life is all about accepting who you are and loving who you are, as far as I'm concerned. I don't care what age, sex, race or weight you are. It doesn't matter to me. The most important thing is that you feel good about yourself.

sunday 25 april
Back in Los Angeles

• **MARVIN** Rochelle arrived today. I've been really missing her, so it's brilliant that she's flown out to see me, even if it is only for four days!

• **ASTON** I've got DVD-itis at the moment. If I see a DVD now, I buy it. The pile is getting bigger and bigger. I've also got my Xbox, PlayStation and a Wii, so anytime I get bored, I can play them, or I listen to music or put some instrumentals on and write tracks. These are the things you do when you don't have a girlfriend!

Although I miss having a girlfriend, I'm not sure if I could handle it right now. Sometimes I do want one, and then I don't. Someone has to really make me want to sweep them off their feet before it happens, I guess.

We've just spent a week promoting 'Everybody In Love' all over the east side of America and a bit in the centre and down

Hhhmmm?!

south. Obviously it's a big place and there's a lot more to do, but everybody's started to pick up on the single now and we're very excited about people's reaction to it. Hopefully, we'll be able to capitalise on that and people all over the country will get to know it.

We've met loads of stars – we bumped into Eva Longoria coming out of a restaurant the other week. She is absolutely incredible! It was love at first sight for me. We also saw Mekhi Phifer from *8 Mile*; Britney Spears walked past JB and Marvin on her way to the spa in our hotel; and Muse were standing outside when we arrived.

• **ORITSÉ** It's a great change of scene and environment, but I miss our English fans, although it's amazing to see that people are starting to get to know us here.

• **MARVIN** The radio tour has been pretty grounding and humbling; it makes us appreciate everything we have back home because nobody knows who we are here. It's great spending time with the boys. We're working very hard because we're starting from the bottom again, but we're not afraid of hard work.

• **ORITSÉ** It's two extremes. Here, we're working from the ground up. There's no TV show to boost us, our music has to speak for itself. It's a tougher journey, but it's one that I've always dreamed of since I was a kid. I'm not worried because as long as we keep working hard and believing in ourselves, I'm certain that everything will fall into place in its natural time.

Our RiDER, How Rock & Roll!!

EPILOGUE

So that's where this part of our story draws to an end, at the start of the second phase of our incredible journey. It's been wicked keeping a diary; it has kept us focused on our fans and helped us to take in all the amazing things we've been doing, which can sometimes get lost in a blur as life gets faster and faster. We hope you enjoyed reading it as much as we enjoyed writing it! Here's where we sign off – until the next time . . .

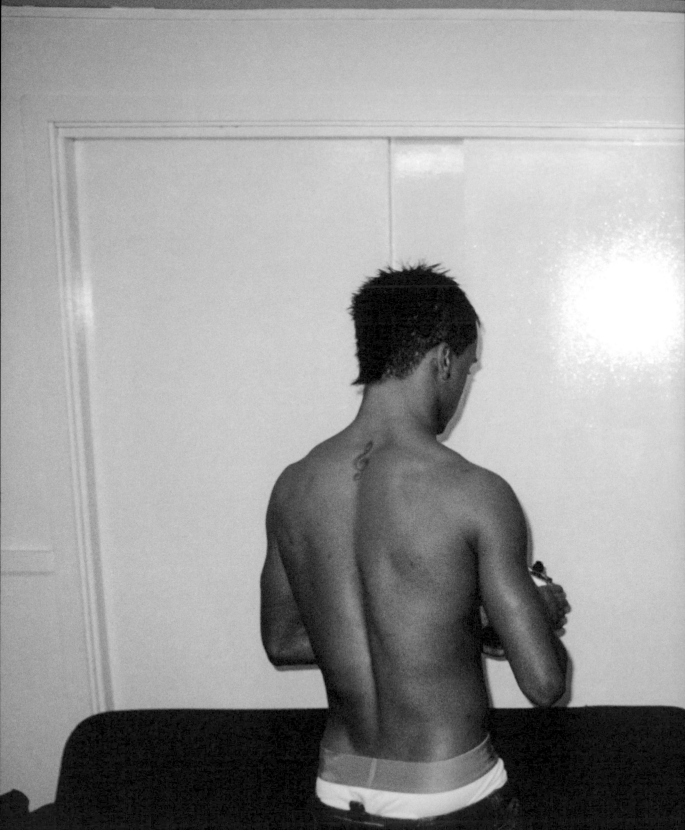

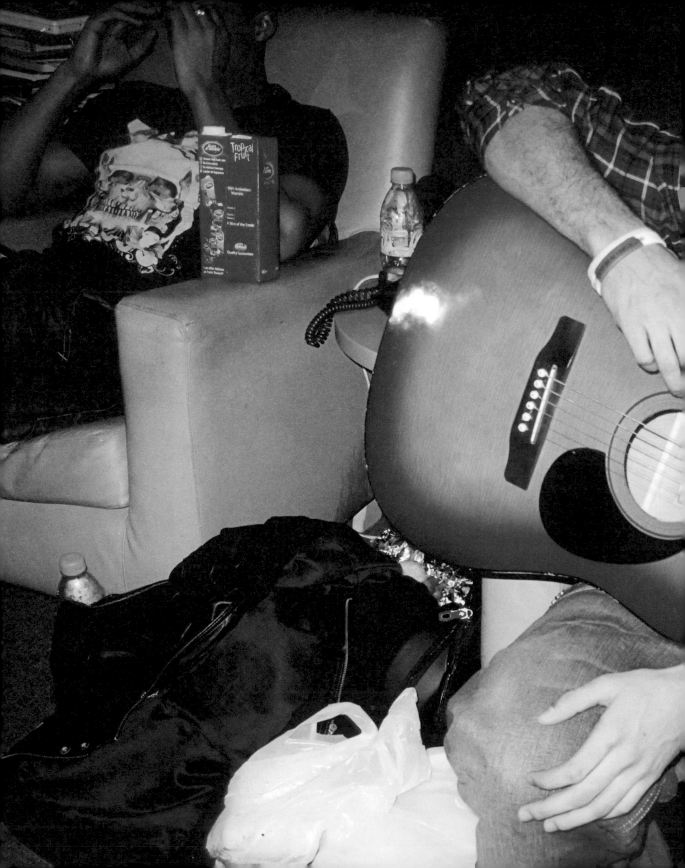

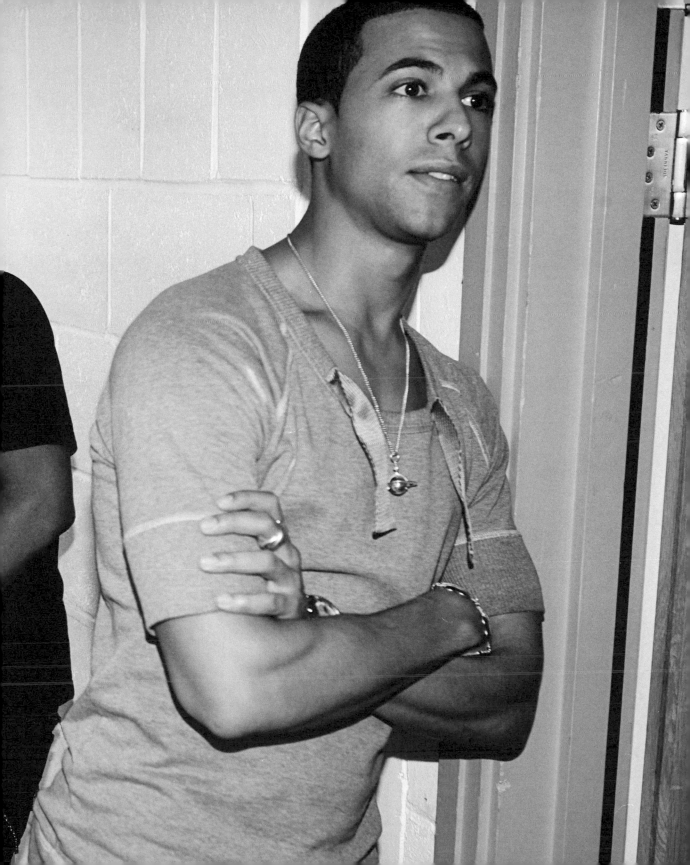

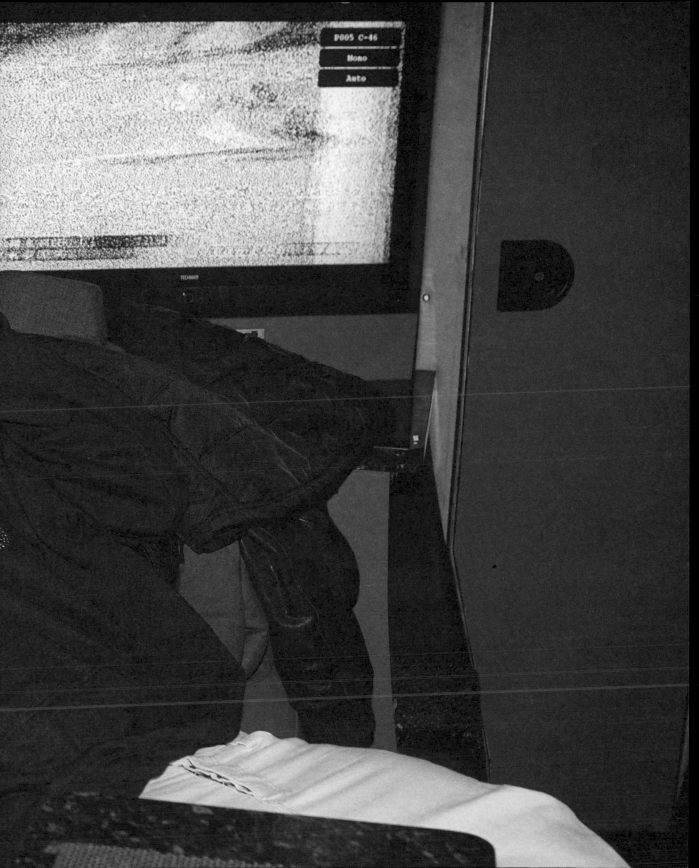

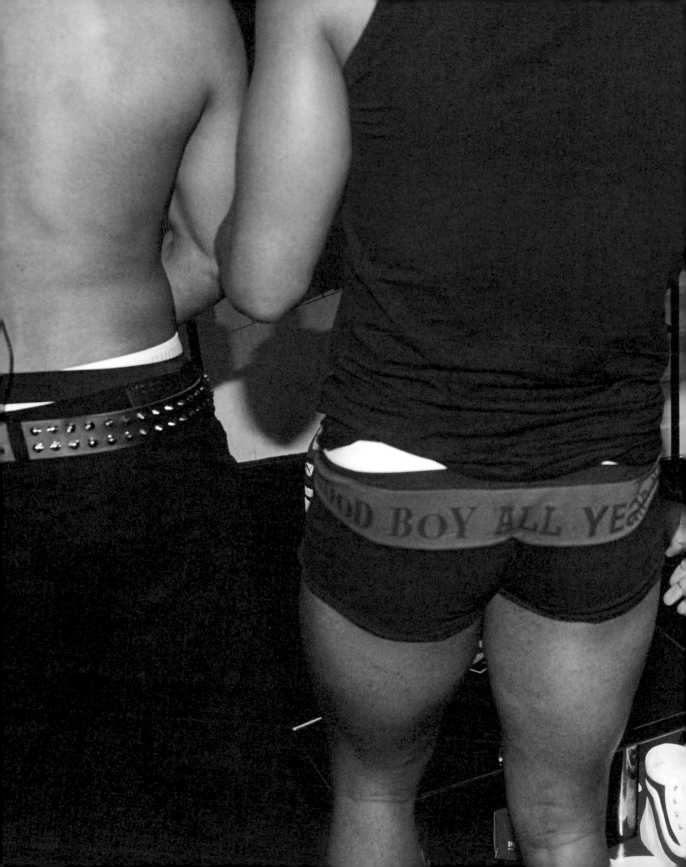

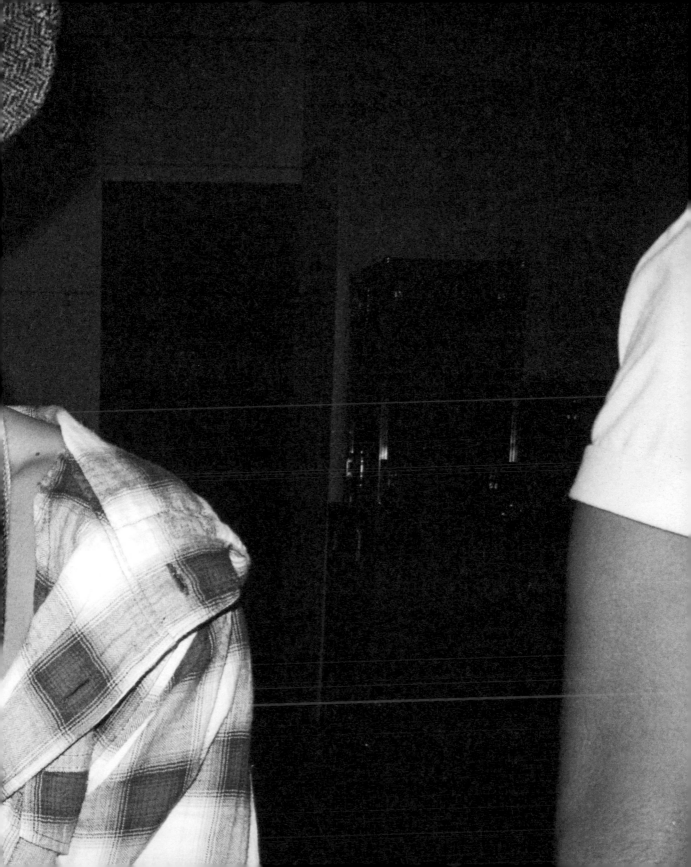

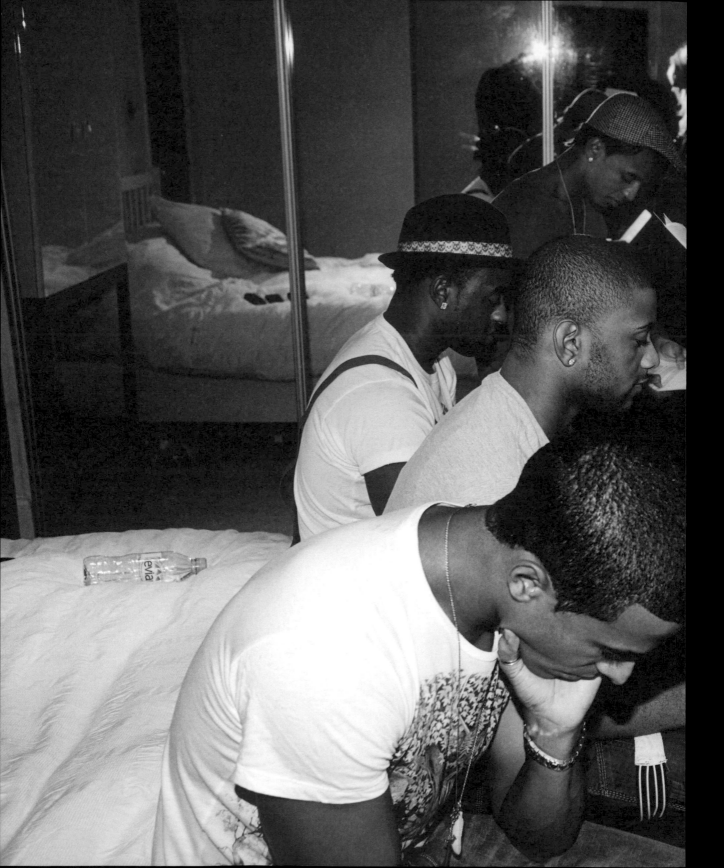

BROTHERS IN ARMS, AAAHHH!! BROMANCE!!!

Wow, it's kind of crazy to be doing this a second time around! A big thanks must go to everybody who has helped with the success of our first book, *JLS – Our Story So Far*. Thanks to you all – we are extremely proud to be in a position to publish our second JLS book. A huge thanks as always to Mr Dean Freeman who has, yet again, been instrumental in the production of this book, as well as Joby and Rebecca. Thanks to all at HarperCollins for their continued belief in JLS. To Modest! Management; Richard, Harry and Phil. Alexi Cory-Smith and all at Lee and Thompson solicitors. Thank you guys for taking care of the necessaries on our behalf. We know that you are just as responsible for making this happen as anybody else. Also, to our 'glam squad', Lucy Manning and Ellie Stidolph, Michael Green and Michael Gray, thanks again for making us look incredible at every opportunity, we love you! Finally to our families and our supporters, we love you unconditionally. Thank you for supporting us with the same unconditional love, thoughts and prayers, day in and day out. We dedicate this book to you.

JB, MARVIN, ORITSE and ASTON x

JLS are represented exclusively by Richard Griffiths and Harry Magee for Modest! Management.

Modest!

Dean Freeman is the publishing agent and consultant to Modest!/JLS on this book; he is also the creative director and photographer. Dean has published eight books, many of them best-sellers on stars of music and sport, and he is an internationally renowned photographer.

'Freeman captures a sense of urgency and immediacy, creating a need to look and see his images. His photography has a sense of humour and an appreciation for the absurd, but where Freeman truly excels is in detecting the beauty that extends beyond time and place.' Nylon Magazine

Dean would like to thank JLS for their energy, talent, warmth and enthusiasm. Also Modest! Management – as ever a great team, and tour manager Adam Lambert, Richard Poulton Digital and Amanda Masters – thanks for the use of your wonderful home in Hollywood.

EXCLUSIVE ACCESS

You've read the private diaries of JLS, now see the brand new content created just for you.

Oritsé, Marvin, Aston and JB invite you to watch the behind-the-scenes action from the cover shoot for this book. As well as this, there's a video of the boys revealing all, as they answer a selection of questions from you, their fans. Plus some gorgeous never-before-seen photos.

To view this new exclusive content, simply peel the sticker off the front of this book to reveal your own personal access code, then visit **www.jlsbook.com** where you enter the code.

HarperCollins*Publishers*
77–85 Fulham Palace Road,
Hammersmith, London W6 8JB

www.harpercollins.co.uk

First published by HarperCollins*Publishers* in 2010

10 9 8 7 6 5 4 3 2 1

Creative direction/photography/book concept by Dean Freeman
Designed by Joby Ellis

JLS assert the moral right to be
identified as the authors of this work

A catalogue record of this book is
available from the British Library

ISBN 978-0-00-735945-5

Printed and bound in Great Britain by
Butler Tanner and Dennis Ltd, Frome, Somerset

Mixed Sources
Product group from well-managed
forests and other controlled sources
www.fsc.org Cert no. SW-COC-001806
© 1996 Forest Stewardship Council
FSC

FSC is a non-profit international organisation established to promote the
responsible management of the world's forests. Products carrying the FSC
label are independently certified to assure consumers that they come
from forests that are managed to meet the social, economic and
ecological needs of present and future generations.

Find out more about HarperCollins and the environment at
www.harpercollins.co.uk/green